Surrounded by Mystery

Other Books by Ruth Senter

Startled by Silence
  Finding God in Unexpected Places
Secrets from Ordinary Places
  Finding God in the Every Day
Seasons of Friendship
So You're a Pastor's Wife

Surrounded by Mystery

Finding God In the Contradictions Of Faith

RUTH SENTER

Zondervan Publishing House
Grand Rapids, Michigan

SURROUNDED BY MYSTERY
Copyright © 1988 by Ruth Senter

Daybreak Books are published by Zondervan Publishing House,
1415 Lake Drive, S.E., Grand Rapids, Michigan 49506

Library of Congress Cataloging in Publication Data

Senter, Ruth Hollinger, 1944–
  Surrounded by mystery.

  "Daybreak Books."
    1. Meditations. 2. Senter, Ruth Hollinger,
1944– .   I. Title.
BV4832.S46 1988   242   87-31440
ISBN 0-310-38871-6

All Scripture quotations, unless otherwise noted, are taken from the HOLY
BIBLE: NEW INTERNATIONAL VERSION (North American Edition),
copyright © 1973, 1978, 1984 by the International Bible Society. Used by
permission of Zondervan Bible Publishers.

Edited by Julie Ackerman Link

Printed in the United States of America

90 91 92 93 94 95 / ML / 10 9 8 7 6 5 4 3 2

The measure
of a mature mind
is the ability to hold
contradictory thoughts simultaneously.

—Thomas Carlyle

Contents

CHAPTER ONE

The Mystery
of Freedom

A Just God

I watch the sun filter through the ancient oaks of Wisconsin's glaciated Kettle Moraine area. The early morning light slips silently from branch to branch. The couple in the neighboring tent watches the same sunrise through bleary eyes, accompanied by pulsing vibes from a ghetto blaster.

"They couldn't be more than sixteen," I say to Mark as we climb the hill for water. We both doubt the legitimacy of their night together in the Coleman tent. But the sun, that celestial goddess of all Wisconsin campers, shines just as brightly on their side of the ancient oaks as it does on ours. And hours later, when the moisture gathers into cumulonimbus and the heavens descend, we are pelted just as hard with the driving rain. Never mind that I'd just spent thirty minutes studying the book of Isaiah while the neighbors guzzled more beer and

rocked to the Beatles. "God is fair," I say to myself as I
walk away, "whether I understand his ways or not." For
nature—that neutral agent of distribution—shows no
partiality (see Matthew 5:45).

Neither does pain. Today I ride my bike down the
street to the gold house on the corner of Thunderbird and
Blackhawk. Death sits in this place. I feel it as soon as I
step inside. Beth's wheelchair is folded by the door, and
her cane hangs on the closet doorknob.

"She's too weak to even use them anymore," her
mother volunteers. "We haven't walked in a week."

Tears gather in her blue eyes, and I try to swallow the
tightness in my throat. I try to make it all go away,
including this ugly nightmare of an inoperable brain tumor
that sucks life from a fourteen-year-old, but I can't. I
notice the family picture that hangs above the livingroom
couch. It shows Beth nine months ago—a track star in full
bloom. But now the petals are shriveling; the flowers are
fading.

"Beth talks about heaven," her mother says. "And the
neighbors are asking how this could happen to us because
we go to church every Sunday."

"God is fair," I say to myself as I walk away, "whether
I understand his ways or not." And pain—that neutral
agent of distribution—falls on the just and the unjust.

I see the sun rise. I feel the rain fall. And I witness the
impartiality of it all. No respecter of persons. Why should I
expect anything different? Nature reflects the one who
created it. God is just; he shows no partiality. Outside of
grace, sin's penalty falls on all. "For the wages of sin is
death" (Romans 6:23). Sin is sin. The consequences have
been posted. God gives fair warning. No excuses. Rebellion, be it active or passive, calls for justice.

I understand God's justice because I remember rebellion—ten-year-old rebellion. My father dispensed the justice. "No swimming in the creek today." His ultimatum was simple, but I had plenty of excuses. "Jimmy went in." "I was so hot." "Everybody else's dads let them go." Excuses didn't matter; I had violated the standard. The penalty was swift and sure. Justice was done.

But then the father who administered justice reached for his big white handkerchief and wiped tears from his eyes. That day, justice and love were forever linked in my mind.

As I reflect on the paradox of love and justice, I remember where my lessons began.

My father's actions pointed me toward a heavenly Father who sits in the hall of justice, calls his creation to accountability, but weeps over waywardness even as he pronounces the sentence. " 'Oh, Jerusalem, Jerusalem . . . how often I have longed to gather your children together, as a hen gathers her chicks under her wings, but you were not willing'!" (Luke 13:34).

Justice and love in the same person.

The sun rises on both sides of the camp. Rain falls on the tents of the godly and the ungodly. Sin contaminates all, but grace is available to all. I can be at peace about God's system of justice for I have confidence in the judge.

As a sinner who found grace, I know God, not as a judge, but as a loving father who continually calls me to accountability. One day he was my judge, but I also see him with a handkerchief as he weeps over my rebellion, issues my sentence, and then takes my penalty upon himself. I am acquitted. Justice has been done.

Somewhere in Wisconsin, the sun still shines on the tents of the ungodly, and down the street a fourteen-year-old withers away. "God is fair," I say to myself, "whether I understand his ways or not. For he is a God of justice."

Fences

When we moved to our new home ten years ago, backyards stretched uninterrupted for the entire block. Kids ran the full length of the village green. No one worried about boundaries. Neighbors could cut across backyards without the hassle of fence-jumping and the guilt of trespassing.

Then came the age of the fence. I'm not sure who came up with the idea, but someone decided a picket fence would enhance the neighborhood. One by one the yards took shape. Full picket. Split picket. White picket. Split rail. Chain link. Batten board.

Not long after the fences sprang up, I noticed a strange backyard phenomenon. Up and down "the strip," neighbors gathered by their fences to talk. Some leaned into conversation, elbows resting. Others hugged the posts with a full-hand grip. Some rested their feet on lower rails.

Others propped their backs against board and batten. Never before had news flowed so freely. Looking out my back door was like witnessing a scene from Robert Frost's "Mending Wall," "'Good fences make good neighbors.'" The fences, confining though they were to our kids, provided a security that promoted adult conversation.

I have never read any behavioral science studies on the sociological implications of a fence, but I sense that they represent the human need for limits. I *have* observed what happens to conversations when they occur *over* something—a fence, table, or teacup. I have also heard about an oddly similar response in sheep. When fenced in, they roam freely over the pasture. Remove the fences and they huddle together in a frightened little clump.

Boundaries. Sometimes they make me feel secure. But sometimes they make me feel restricted. Fence me in and I immediately want freedom. It is my nature. When I had my tonsils removed at age six, I was a fairly peaceful patient until the nurse tried to tie my hands to the side of the operating table. Then I turned into a tiger.

A part of me still resists limits, whether they are diets, speed limits, or God's "Thou shalt nots." If the speed limit is twenty miles per hour, I'm inclined to take the straight stretch at at least thirty. Speed-limit signs and calorie charts remind me of boundaries. God's Word has the same effect.

Freedom is not untied hands, but understanding the value of restraints. I need God's boundaries, just as I need speed-limit signs, to show me the difference between obedience and disobedience. "Through the law," Paul says in Romans 3:20, "we become conscious of sin."

I have learned the need for personal boundaries to keep myself from overload. I know, for example, that one commitment per month outside of home and work is all I can comfortably handle. Defining my boundaries enables me to say no.

I cannot say I enjoy discipline. But I've learned that it provides the security I need to roam the pasture. For freedom, I am learning, is not an absence of limits but a healthy respect for restraint.

The Road Down the Mountain

Paths to the top of this mountain should be one way. No one ever wants to go down. This path leads to the sun—a place of peace and tranquility.

The glory of the Lord breathes in every lodgepole pine and giant fir up here. It stretches all the way to the glacier fields and pours itself over the rocks, tumbling downward in watery crescendo. It passes over the alpine flowers, and far below it reflects the aqua blue of the mountain lake. We have climbed so far I feel almost celestial.

Viewed from this pinnacle of majesty, life below takes on different meaning. Why do the heathen rage and the humans rush to and fro, frantically chasing their tails? What are those specks of dust that build castles in the sand and then watch them wash away with the first big rain?

Life in the clouds gives perspective. Authenticity. Simplicity. A log cabin provides our shelter, and a helicopter delivers our daily bread. We fill our cups from glacier runoff and breathe deeply of nature's pure air. No one wears a watch; there's no reason to look at one. We feed the ground creatures—the chipmunks and the marmots—and talk to the white-breasted grosbeak that sits on our table.

Surely this is hallowed ground. I can worship in this place. We write poems about majesty in our journals. We read about majesty. "O LORD, our Lord, how majestic is your name in all the earth! You have set your glory above the heavens" (Psalm 8:1). We sing about majesty. "O Lord my God, when I in awesome wonder, consider all the worlds thy hands have made . . ." We write about insignificance. "What is man that you are mindful of him?" (Psalm 8:4).

"Peter said to Jesus, 'Lord, it is good for us to be here. If you wish, I will put up shelters'" (Matthew 17:4). But Jesus pointed Peter to the path down the mountain. As they went, Jesus instructed them about his suffering which was soon to come.

"God is a presence, not a place," I say to myself as I head down the mountain.

Once home I find a friend in the hospital, a neighbor who is dying, and a man who is drunk, depressed, and reaching out for help. "God is a presence, not a place," I repeat to myself. And so I look at the photographs of my moments on the mountain, remember what God did for me there, but reluctantly agree to live life on the plains.

Safe Within the Limits

I am caught in conformity
   To this interstate
   To the flow of traffic around me.
I read the speed limit signs
But the miles per hour
Creep up on me
A little at a time.
I simply go with the flow
Of U-Hauls and gray Subarus.

Safe standard, I suppose,
Since they can read signs too.
So I clock myself by the crowd—
A conveyor belt of commuter traffic
Accustomed to traveling by its own speed limits.
"The law is broken only if you get caught."
We travel thus,
Until the blue light flashes,
And justice demands its due.

But
I have another way of setting a standard.
I push a small black button by my steering wheel
That sets the pace
Within the limits.

It relieves me of the competition—
    "That truck is passing me again."
The ambiguity—
    "Wonder how fast he is going."
The dread of the law—
    "Was that a squad car I saw?"

I sit back and enjoy the ride—
Safe within control.

Lord,
Your Word is my cruise control.
    It governs my speed
    Checks my excesses
    Restrains my impulses.
May I not forget to use it
So that I can sit back and enjoy the ride
Safe within your limits.

Measuring-Stick Spirituality

"How am I doing, Mom?" ten-year-old Nicky asks every third day or so. He's usually comparing the top of his head with the marks on the garage wall or with some landmark on his mother. What kid doesn't like to watch himself get taller? What ten-year-old doesn't measure himself next to his mother or red marks on the garage wall?

Personal yardsticks are signs of growing up, but not necessarily signs of growing mature. Growth can be an obsession—a measuring-stick mania.

"My husband is the spiritual standard in our house," I once heard a wife say. "Next to him, I feel like a shrimp."

What is this thing called spirituality, I began to wonder. Something we wear like a gold chain around the neck? Something we do like a household chore? Something we either have or don't have—like blond hair and blue eyes? Something we add or subtract and tally up on a scorecard?

"How do you recognize a spiritual person?" Mark asked a group of high schoolers one day.

Doug's answers never came quickly, but when they came we paid attention. "I don't think you know a spiritual person until they're gone." He didn't elaborate. He'd said enough, and I have spent years digesting his thought.

Philosopher George Santayana, in his book *The Birth of Reason and Other Essays*, states, "Health is not conscious of itself, but frees the mind for the perception of other things . . ."

Spiritual health is no exception. If I had to pinpoint spirituality in human form, I would say that it probably exists to the greatest measure in the one who is least aware of it. For spirituality, it seems to me, does not focus on *me* but on *God*. It asks not "How am *I* doing?" but "What will *you* have me do?"

Growth is not a plan we follow, a formula we calculate, a manual we study. "Which of you by taking thought can add one cubit unto his stature?" (Matthew 6:27 KJV), Jesus asked during his Sermon on the Mount.

I do not see spiritual growth happen in my life any more than my ten-year-old sees himself add an inch or a pound.

Spiritual growth is not an act of the mind. I cannot think myself more spiritual any more than Nick can think himself two inches taller. He does not grow by watching growth charts but by eating his Cheerios and drinking his milk, by getting eight hours of sleep each night, and by playing soccer twice a week. Growth is a by-product of healthy living.

So it is with the spirit. Spiritual growth is the by-product of communion with God. Understanding this, I can put away my spiritual yardstick, for communion with God is a thing of the heart. Others may be aware of its absence in my life, but not necessarily conscious of its presence.

Spirituality does not draw attention to itself. Like air, it is necessary for life but invisible. You seldom think of it when it's present, but you know immediately when it's missing.

Others will see signs of growth, though. "My, how you've grown," Grandma usually says to Nick when she sees him every six months or so. The fact is, Nick has grown, and you can't help but notice the difference.

The same is true in the spiritual realm: The condition of one's heart is lived out in actions. Right actions naturally follow right thinking. But communion with God, not right actions, is the goal.

I look for an example, and I remember the one perfect embodiment of spirituality. Though not always recognized as he walked this earth, when he was gone, soldiers trembled and said, "Truly this was the Son of God" (Matthew 27:54 KJV). His walk with the Father was so close that he did not consider how he was doing on the spirituality polls. But when he was gone, people knew they had been in the presence of spiritual greatness.

Joy

Is it joy—
This ray of sunshine
That splashes itself over my front porch swing
   Where mounds of raspberry-colored pillows
   Are wrapped in summertime gold?
That reaches beyond to the crab apple
   Where the cardinal sings?

Does joy
Ride high above the amusement park
Where fun comes packaged
   In swirling cages,
   Pink cotton candy on a stick,
   And sailboat rides across the bay?

Or does joy
Leap from the pages of my ledger book
When all the bills are paid
And the green flows freely,
   Spit from some invisible reservoir
   Through a slot in the bank lobby wall?

Joy?
Perhaps it is my name
On the title page of a hardcover book
On credentials framed and hanging on an oak-paneled wall
Or printed on a four-color flyer
    Announcing the topic of my speech.

But does joy
Drip down the front porch swing
And run into little rivulets of mud
From the four-day rain,
    Turning raspberry-colored pillows to sog?

Joy?
An amusement park closed for the season,
Shuttered in motionless gray.
Like a great prehistoric monster,
The Screaming Eagle is encased in ice.
The thrill is gone.

Joy?
Bank account spent
While
Letters in white envelopes
    Demand payment for services rendered
    Or college tuition by the first of the month.

Joy?
When the only one who reads my name is the mailman
Who also brings letters addressed to 'Occupant'
Announcing this season's sale on garbage cans
And three-quarter-inch nails.

Nails rust; garbage cans leak.
And who knows
When the season's sales will start or end?

But as for joy
It is always and forever
A single thought:
Thank you, Lord, for
    Soggy pillows

My name—known only to the mailman
And the season's sale on three-quarter-inch nails.

For joy is
Thanksgiving
When there's nothing much to be thankful for.

The Trouble with Strings
(A Parable About Freedom)

Like all kites, I have a basic need to fly. That's why hanging on a nail beside the furnace all winter made me so restless. "This isn't what I was made for," I'd say to the furnace as much as to anyone. "I need to fly. I have to fly. Kites were made for skies, not walls."

I endured those wall-hanging months by thinking of flying days to come. I pictured the wide open spaces of blue. I felt the powerful lift of the wind. I smelled freedom. "That'll be the life," I'd say to the furnace as much as to anyone. "No more basement blues for me. I'll find fulfillment in gliding to new heights. I'll show my power by soaring. I'll find freedom in drifting wherever I please. That's what real living is all about."

Spring finally arrived, and with it came billowing breezes and crisp blue skies that beckoned me to join them. I'm now doing what kites are meant to do—glide, soar, drift. If this is living, my spirits should be soaring.

But they're not.

I've decided it's the string. My problem is all wrapped up in this string.

I glide 500 feet above the yards, trees, and houses, but I can go no higher. The string holds me down. My spirit urges, "Go higher." But the string is always there.

I look down on the yards, trees, and houses, but they are always the same. The string holds me back. My spirit whispers, "Go farther." But the string is always there.

I look beyond the yards, trees, and houses, but I cannot reach the fields and meadows I see. The string holds me back. My spirit whispers, "Go alone." But the string is always there.

There was a time I needed the string. When I could hardly get off the ground, it got me up in the air and allowed me to fly. I needed all the help I could get, then. And the string was always there. There was a time when I didn't know direction or control. I needed the string then, too. And when the empty skies looked big and frightening, the string gave me security. There was a time when I didn't know how to land, but the string always guided me gently in. The string has kept me from lots of tragedies, I admit.

But I am experienced now. The skies no longer threaten me. I am confident. I know control and direction. Now I need fulfillment and freedom, not security.

There's so much I've not yet seen. So many places I've not visited. So many things I've not done. My world is so small. I've been so sheltered. The same cold basement walls. The same smelly furnace. The same old houses, yards, and trees. A kite needs to experience new places, new skies, new climates. A kite needs to fly higher and try new tricks. But the string is always there.

How much can a kite do with a string tied to it? How creative can a kite be when the person holding the string just stands on the ground gripping it tightly with both hands? How much of a kite am I if I allow the string-holder to keep tugging me right or left or pulling me in? How can I ever develop my own flying skills? How can I find fulfillment when I'm tied to a string?

"What I need is freedom," I said one day, as much to the furnace as to anyone. "I need to be my own kite, to do my own thing. Then I would really soar. Then I'd learn to feel, to experience, to grow. Strings are restricting," I added in disgust.

I would never be mature until I called my own shots. When I reached new heights, I would be wiser as to the ways of the atmosphere. When I got beyond my own house, yard, and trees, I would better understand other kites. When I made my own flight plan I'd be able to handle other decisions as well. "It would all be very educational for me as a kite," I said to the furnace as much as to anyone.

And then my big chance came. The call of the skies was louder. The pull of the wind was stronger. The smell of freedom was more enticing. But the string was there as usual, guiding me first to the left, then to the right, up over the trees, the house, and the yard. As usual, the string kept coming, a little at a time, just as I needed it. But I knew this was my chance to break free.

The big gust caught me as I was gliding about 500 feet up. I pulled with all my might. At last, freedom.

I don't remember anything after that.

Anyone know how to fix a broken kite?

CHAPTER TWO

The Mystery
of Silence

The Bridge to Silence

The world has been stripped of words. I park my car at the far end of the lane that bridges the river and walk to a quiet retreat center. River sounds and bird sounds greet me as I walk, but the only human welcome I receive is from a nun at the entrance. "God bless your day of quiet" is all she says as she hands me my room key. Her smile says the rest.

Silence follows me down the narrow hallways and turns the corner with me into room number eight, which faces the woods. The room has no TV or radio, no books in the desk drawers, no signs on the walls.

Here in this room with no noise, I wonder at the vacancy. I am not used to a world without words. The verbal barrage of the six o'clock morning news wakens me. Words partition my day and fill up the spaces in between. Instructions to my children. Information for my husband.

Notations on my schedule. Messages over the phone. Slogans on billboards. Letters punched into my computer, spit out by a printer. Words exchanged over a piece of Frango mint pie. Ideas and opinions bartered like soybeans and silver on a commodities exchange.

But today, a day without words, I feel a certain loss. The silence rings in my ears like the ocean in a seashell. What does one do without words? I have come here to think, to study, to pray. Today I do not have to do anything on the run. I am not sure how to act.

I watch a thrush pick through the January snow in search of food. He doesn't come up with even as much as a berry. I wonder if he will survive until spring. Birds intrigue me. At home, bird books line my shelves, and bird pictures hang on my walls. I have three birdfeeders outside my kitchen window. But at home I never have time to wonder about birds. So today I sit and watch and wonder. The thrush is oblivious to time. And watching him today leaves me feeling nourished, not guilty for wasting precious moments.

The day ticks by with muted precision. I listen to my watch and read a devotional book. At lunch I try to decide what to do for the silent strangers who sit on either side of me as we eat our cottage cheese and fruit. I pass them the salt and pepper and feel a bit better. The rest of the time we listen to Vivaldi's *The Four Seasons*, watch the woods, and think. Someone pours hot coffee from my left and sets a bowl of rice pudding in front of me. I turn to say thanks, but the server is already gone.

Words are assumed, not spoken. We linger over the last drop of coffee. No one seems in a hurry to leave so I sit too. I can think of few times when I have sat with others and said nothing. I wouldn't want to be considered a wallflower. But today, it doesn't matter. As I walk back to my room I feel revived, even stimulated, not by conversation but by silent community. Perhaps I've sometimes missed community because of the noise.

Perhaps I've even missed the message because of the noise. When the carillon chimes afternoon vespers, I walk to the chapel, where silence writes its sermon on the velvet tapestry above the altar. "Thank you, O Lord, for your mysteries. For the wonder of myself and the wonder of your work." No choral anthem repeats the theme, and no one expounds on its meaning. So I sit and think about mystery while the afternoon sun creates shadows over the gilded letters.

I am surrounded by mystery. I do not understand sun rays, shadows, or gilded letters, but I praise the effect. I do not understand the ways of God, but I can praise him. I think of Beth, Jori's best friend from junior high who is being eaten alive by a brain tumor. Beth's life has no sun, no gilded letters, not even shadow. Sight, hearing, and speech are gone.

Thank you, O Lord, for your mysteries? To understand God I would have to unravel his mysteries, and to do so would reduce him to my finite level of understanding. So today I am at peace with mystery. I don't need to understand God to praise him.

No words have been spoken but I have heard much. Arsenius, the fifth-century Roman educator who exchanged his status and wealth for the solitude of the Egyptian desert, once said, "I have often repented of having spoken, but never of having remained silent."

I remember his words as I drive through evening toward home. The silence was not always comfortable, but I will not regret having been silent. For if I keep talking, I may end up with nothing to say.

Liquid Gold

Black giraffes
On iron legs
Drink of the crude earth,
Suck liquid life from its veins.
Mechanical haunches
Squat and strain
Dipping beneath
Crusty layers
Drawing energy—
Pipeline to Alaska.

I drive through Oklahoma
Down avenues of derricks
And I reflect on man's ingenious
Attempts to tap the Creator.
I stand on the shores
Of Lake Maracaibo—
Pool of Venezuelan wealth.
Offshore oil rigs rise like
Manhattan on water.
I reflect on my feeble attempts
To draw from my Creator.
"Wells of Salvation—"
Pipeline to the Spirit—
Wait for my rig
While the earth oozes
Liquid gold,
Mine for the drilling.
Amazing,
That I so often
Forget about my resources.

Rainy Nights and
Wooden Crosses

We've come away from the cross. In our sleek, so-phisticated society we allow no time for plain wooden planks that meet in the middle. I read *Architectural Digest* and *National Geographic* magazines, but I don't pay much attention to symbols that dominated the eve of Passover 2000 years ago. I feed my children, shop for groceries, put gas in my car, and drive to the post office, but I don't think much about the Roman style of execution and rocky hillsides shaped like skulls. Life is much too modern for archaic sentimentality.

But tonight calls to the past. My past. His past. Everyman's past. I slip into the semi-dark cathedral. One dim light from somewhere high in the vaulted ceiling makes me barely aware of muted figures passing by me as though in stocking feet. No one talks. Only the Gregorian chant from the far corner of the long, gothic nave breaks the silence. We never see the singers. They slip in and out by a side door.

All eyes focus on a simple crossbeam suspended high above the altar. The light from above shines directly on the cross. Otherwise, all is dark. There is no preacher. No Scripture text. No stained-glass windows.

"The Word was made flesh and lived among us for awhile . . ." The chant goes on, echoing off the vaulted ceiling. What does it mean to me—these simple wooden planks that meet in the middle?

I am in the middle of a fast-paced, upwardly mobile metropolis. But tonight I stop, study the cross, and kneel in shame for so quickly forgetting. This cross, like a wedding band, bonds me forever in love. I am loved. I am loved enough for Roman execution and a rocky, skull-shaped hill.

"Now let thy servant depart in peace . . ." The choir voice grows soft. The light dims. The muted forms around me start to move. I cast one last glance at the hanging wood and know I must return again and again. What tragedy to wander from the cross.

I pull my coat around me and head out into a rainy Seattle night. Returning to the cross compels me also to leave it, because the cross points me outward, to the world. I am loved, yes, but so are they. I see the lights of a million people in the city below. What tragedy should they miss the cross. I must return to the cross for their sakes, as well as for mine.

How Silently?

Silent night . . .
> "But the crowds cried out,
> 'Crucify him. Crucify him.' "

Holy night . . .
> "Then they spat in his face and
> struck him with their fists.
> Others slapped him and said,
> 'Prophecy to us, Christ. Who
> hit you?' "

All is calm . . .
> "When Pilate saw . . . that
> an uproar was starting, he took
> water and washed his hands . . .
> 'I am innocent of this man's blood.'
> All the people answered,
> 'Let his blood be on
> us and on our children.' "

All is bright . . .
> "And darkness came over the

whole land until the ninth hour,
for the sun stopped shining.
And the curtain of the temple
was torn in two.''

Round yon virgin, mother and child . . .
"Who is my mother, and who
are my brothers? . . . From now
on . . . family divided against
each other . . .''

Holy infant . . .
"And carrying his own cross, he
went out to the place of the
skull.''

So tender and mild . . .
"And he cried with a loud voice,
'My God, my God. Why have you
forsaken me?' ''

Sleep . . .
"Foxes have holes and birds of
the air have nests, but the Son
of man has no place to lay his
head.''

In heavenly peace . . .
"Do you think I came to bring
peace to the earth? I did not
come to bring peace, but a
sword.''

Sleep in heavenly peace.
" 'It is finished.' With that,
he bowed his head and gave up
his spirit.''

"And we beheld his glory, the glory
of the one and only Son.''

Too Much of a Good Thing

It has not always been evil that has troubled me the most. Sometimes, it has been good things out of control. The wind becomes the hurricane. The river, the rage.

I stand today and look at such a river, a gentle creek gone wild. I have followed the creek through the seasons, felt the changes in its foliated banks: dormant branch, pregnant bud, full bloom. We have been one, the creek and I, in our stages, and I have found solace in my daily walks along its path.

But today I do not know this creek. Like an invading army, it ignores its boundaries, turns streets into swirling masses of sewer and mud, ravages homes, and holds inhabitants captive.

Motorboats take to the streets as though navigating the canals of Venice. They rescue residents—mostly mothers and children—from the four-feet-deep waters of this out-of-control creek.

Several days later, I walk by the creek again. This time it is contained, quiet, like a sleeping child, giving the illusion of goodness. But evidence of its excesses are everywhere. For as far as I can see, lush, green carpets have turned brittle, scrub-brush brown. Trees drip matted slush, and the air smells like dead fish.

I cross the bridge and walk to the street, where giant, yellow machines bulldoze water-sogged belongings into garbage dumpsters. Months, years, life-times of possessions trashed together in a mournful heap. I notice the mud-streaked face of a doll dangling limply over the top of a brown leather suitcase. I hold my breath as I pass this sewage reservoir of things. I say sadly to myself, "All because of a creek gone wild."

Who would guess that this peaceful meander of blue held so much potential for devastation? And who would guess that the good in our lives, when uncontrolled, can be our own worst enemy?

Why is this so? Perhaps because we build reinforcements only against obvious danger. We do not guard against the good. We sleep by the creek. It is harmless, gentle, peaceful, and restorative to the soul. We relax in good times, good friends, good things. But good things without restraint—good things in excess—may take a lifetime of cleanup.

Paul wrote to the young pastor Timothy, "Guard the *good* deposit that was entrusted to you" (2 Timothy 1:14, italics added).

If we had realized that good creeks could destroy us, perhaps we would not be suffering so today.

Thanks, Lord

My price tag was high.

You reached down deep
        Into your resources.
        It cost you blood.
                You gave me value.

You lifted my head
        And said,
        Walk tall and straight,
        You have nothing to feel guilty about.
                You freed me.

You said,
        See that mountain,
        You can climb it.
        See those rapids,
        You can cross them.
        You have nothing to be timid about.
                You inspired me.

You said,
        See your feet,
        They're made of clay.
        You're human;
        I'm God.
                You gave me perspective.

The China That Stayed in Boxes

Brown masking tape crumbled like parchment under our fingers, and the yellow newspaper wrapping reminded us of fifteen-year-old news. Until that moment I never knew my mother had good china. But there it was in front of me, box after box of English Spode, white etched in delicate pink and trimmed in gold. Before the end of that sultry August afternoon in my grandpa's attic, we had unpacked twelve boxes of my mother's wedding treasures. I had spent fifteen years of my life eating black-eyed peas and turnip greens from plain fiesta plates—colorful but definitely everyday—while cardboard boxes stored the good dishes in an attic a thousand miles away.

"I put them aside for a while," my mother said as she unwrapped a covered soup tureen. "They didn't seem to fit down there." She nodded toward the south, her eyes misty. I knew how much she loved the poor cotton-farming families she'd left behind in the small communities of southern Alabama. She and Daddy had spent thirteen years of their lives in rural mission work.

Mother's packed dishes preached a sermon I've never forgotten. While reading Helmut Thielicke's *How to Believe Again*, I thought of her china. Says Thielicke, "When we find God, we are immediately taken into his service, placed on the track of our neighbor, and faced with an absolute demand."

There is no true service without giving up something. Sacrifice *is* an absolute demand. Some may have to set aside china or other signs of the good life. Others may have to empty themselves, as Christ did when he laid aside his rights to royalty (Philippians 2).

Mark Twain, in his novel *The Prince and the Pauper*, tells of the young son of King Henry VIII who changes positions with a poor boy in London. After Edward Tudor, the Prince of Wales, has donned the tattered rags of Tom Canty, he looks at the beggar boy from Offal Court and says, "And now that I am clothed as thou wert clothed, it seemeth I should be able more nearly to feel as thou didst when the brute soldier—hark ye, is not this a bruise upon your hand?"

With those words, the Prince of Wales, wearing beggar clothes, goes out to seek vengeance upon the soldier responsible for the bruise on his new friend's hand. Mistaking the prince for Tom, the soldier boxes his ears so hard that the young noble is sent sprawling to the street.

"Be off, thou crazy rubbish," he says as the jeering crowd closes around the poor little prince and hoots him out of town.

After years of anguish and grief as a poor beggar, the Prince of Wales is restored to his rightful throne, where he reigns mercifully.

Later, when "some gilded vassal of the crown, made argument against his leniency . . . the young king turned the mournful eloquence of his great compassionate eyes upon him and answered: 'What dost *thou* know of suffering and oppression? I and my people know, but not thou.'"

For the Son of God, sacrifice not only involved "laying aside" for the sake of another, but "taking on" the nature of a servant (Philippians 2:7). In an exchanged status, like that in Mark Twain's *The Prince and the Pauper*, lies the mystery of the Incarnation, the greatest act of putting aside and taking on. Christ exchanged royal vesture for humanity's tattered rags, a scepter for a manger, divine insignia for a criminal's cross. He gave up his right to power and reached instead for a towel. "Jesus knew that the Father had put all things under his power . . . so he . . . wrapped a towel around his waist . . . and began to wash his disciples' feet" (John 13:3–5).

I confess, I don't have my good china packed away in cardboard boxes in the attic. I haven't made great sacrificial exchanges or spectacular "putting asides" recently. I know the scramble for status. I have felt the appeal of name recognition and visibility.

But in the midst of a world consumed with what it can acquire—status, china, salaries, or numbers on a church membership roll—I see twelve boxes of English Spode china packed away in Grandpa's attic. I remember the meaning of "putting aside" for the sake of another. I approach God and am confronted with a baby, a manger, a towel, and a cross.

The Difference

I could only see down.
>   You made me look up;
>   I began to notice the world outside myself.

I felt besieged.
>   You melted my defenses;
>   I became approachable.

I cried.
>   You heard;
>   I slept like a baby.

I felt pulled apart.
>   You were my glue;
>   I held together.

I was overwhelmed.
>   You handed me one moment at a time;
>   I relaxed.

CHAPTER THREE

The Mystery
of Love

Life Without Magic

Fairy tales were okay when I was a child. I was captivated by the idea that a plain-clothed kitchen maid could turn into a dazzling Cinderella and command the heart of Prince Charming, who combed the kingdom to find her, then carried her off to a land where they lived happily ever after.

During my formative years, when it came time for me to learn about virtues, fairy tales supplied them. Honor. Strength. (Have you ever read of a prince who *couldn't* slay the dragon?) Loyalty. Courage. The triumph of good. (The wicked witch always loses.) Fairy tales were a fun way to learn difficult truths.

When I grew up, I put my fairy-tale books on the shelf. But adulthood has created its own fantasies for me—especially when it comes to marriage. Madison Avenue hawks its wares: love sold over the counter in a bottle from

Paris; happiness packaged with a weekend rate in Aca-pulco. Moonlight and roses. Candlelight and surf. Idyllic settings.

The prince is always handsome, immaculately groomed, smiling through perfect white teeth as he hoists the sails of his catamaran. Cheap fiction makes bigger-than-life men, always sensitive, warm, and attentive to the needs of the women in their lives. Who wouldn't enjoy such love? If I'm not careful, I fall for the pitch.

Romantic that I am, cold, hard facts don't set well with me. Marriage for me has been learning to adjust to reality. The white horse never came galloping out of the sunset. Instead, our Corvair broke down on the interstate just outside of Baltimore, and my young minister-husband and I spent part of our honeymoon in a garage. During the twenty-three years since our wedding day, Mark and I haven't galloped anywhere. Instead, we've gotten up in the morning and put one foot ahead of the other. My prince charming is fighting a losing battle with a receding hair line, and his noble quest for love is often lost in theology and three-point outlines. We often forget to light the candles before dinner.

Marriage has also been learning to live without magic. No fairy godmother has ever waved her wand over cluttered desks, forgotten grocery lists, or jogging clothes left on the shelf instead of put in the drawers. Magic words have never produced for Mark a wife who can sit down after dinner and watch the news with him instead of rushing off to clean up the kitchen. No kiss has ever transformed my hurried step into a slow and easy stroll. Living without magic is not easy, but I am stronger because I've learned to face reality. I know more about the grace of God in my marriage because I've lived without fantasy.

Marriage for me has also been learning to look for the

good in the one I know best. Men at a distance always look better than the one I see shaving in front of the mirror every morning. Conversation with a male is always easier when we haven't had to unplug the stopped-up kitchen sink, balance the checkbook, or discipline a child. Familiarity blurs my ability to see good in my spouse. I may even stop looking for it because I am so busy looking for happiness.

In a poll conducted by *Psychology Today*, a man married for more than twenty years said, "Commitment means a willingness to be unhappy for a while." Such statements are not good PR for marriage. In fact, I wonder how many fairy tales would have sold had they ended simply "and they lived together ever after." Who doesn't want to be happy? Something would be wrong if I didn't desire a happy marriage.

But Jesus puts happiness in another context. "Blessed [happy] are the peacemakers," he said. Not happy are those who've never known troubles, but happy are those who have learned to bring peace out of the trouble—a foreign idea in fairy tales, where the nobility lives happily only after conflict has been forever banished.

Fairy tales are nice diversions in literature, but they promote an unrealistic view of love and happiness. God looked on his creation and pronounced it good, not easy or happy. And I suppose, despite my love for candlelight and roses and weekends in Acapulco, were you to ask about my marriage I would have to say, "It's been good." And according to God's standard, that's a high tribute.

A Gift Wrapped in Brown Paper

There's a beautiful gift
        inside this package.
It's wrapped for
        protection;
        tied for security.
Stamped: "Fragile!
        Handle With Care!"

It's easy to loosen
        the strings,
to let just anyone
        tear away the
        wrapping,
to give the gift
        without commitment—
or hand it out as the prize
        for winning a game.

There's a gift wrapped
        inside this brown paper.
It's for keeps.
Non-returnable.
It's a surprise,
        a happy treat to be
        opened
        by the person
        to whom it's addressed,
        on the date marked
Forever.

Close-up Distance

I had never seen Mark look more handsome than he did walking onto the platform in his three-piece, dark-gray suit and taking his seat behind the podium.

I know that man, I thought to myself as I watched him standing tall and straight behind the pulpit, leading the congregation in responsive reading. I did know him—the inside Mark.

I could tell by the pitch of his voice whether he felt nervous or calm, by the slope of his shoulders whether he felt discouraged or exhilarated, by what he did with his hands whether he was uptight or relaxed. These external clues of his internal feelings were unknown to all but me— the one who had lived with him for twenty-three years, getting to know what went on inside.

Suddenly the rows between us dissolved. I sensed

Mark's closeness, his presence, our oneness, even though we were isolated from each other by pews of people.

The mystery of marriage, I thought to myself, *is that two people, though separated by distance, can be so close.* The sadness of it all is that two people may be sitting side by side and yet be miles apart.

I know. We were there once, absorbed in the busyness of life around us, caught up in the work of the kingdom, intent on ministering to the hurts and concerns of others.

We were busy doing, growing, learning—about Christian education programs for the church, about strategies for world evangelism, about Christian journalism and interpersonal communication. We taught courses at the graduate school, attended conferences, led seminars, preached sermons.

In the midst of our activity, we always found time to be together, jealously guarding our family hours. Somewhere over the clutter and clatter of life with the children, we would squeeze in a word or two for each other—details of parenting and daily transactions that kept the wheels of a household oiled and running smoothly.

When we dropped exhausted into bed at the end of the day, we would have little left for each other. But we'd say "good night," satisfied by tasks accomplished, people helped, experiences gained, progress made.

Our marriage could have survived that way for a long time. You couldn't say we weren't happily married: we were. We respected each other, were polite and helpful, remembered birthdays and anniversaries, and always called home when one of us was out of town.

On the rare nights we were home together, we'd build a fire in the fireplace after the children were tucked into bed. From behind the pages of a newspaper or a book by C. S. Lewis, Tolstoy, or Solzhenitsyn, we'd share our evenings together. We'd lose ourselves in a world of current events, science fiction, or human drama.

We could have spent a lifetime of evenings that way. In the security of the routine, the functional, the predictable, we probably could have maintained the status quo and played the marriage game indefinitely.

But we didn't. God in his graciousness disrupted our equilibrium. He sent along a counselor-friend and some written tests to show us how little we knew about each other.

We knew a lot about our world, our professions, our children, and about how to serve God's kingdom, but very little about each other's thoughts and feelings.

We had substituted the know-how of marriage for knowing each other. We had exchanged activity for intimacy. We had grown, but not together.

Reawakenings force us to assess our deficiencies. And somewhere in the assessment, we may discover painful truths about ourselves—our bent toward perfectionism and performance, toward activity and productivity, toward the immediate, the urgent. Hidden truths about ourselves keep us from knowing the truths about another.

But with painful reawakening comes joyful discovery—finding what's been missing but always within reach. Fortunately for Mark and me, the discoveries began.

We're learning, for example, to sit and talk to each other, not only at the end of an exhausting day but one morning a week of prime time. Sometimes we find our solitude while enjoying a hot drink at a little pastry shop, away from telephones and children. Sometimes we meet in our living room before dinner, just the two of us.

We try to talk, not about people we've known, places we've been, children we're rearing, but about ourselves and our relationship. We've learned that it's okay to talk about ourselves because doing so unravels for us a baffling and sometimes mind-boggling puzzle—the thoughts and feelings, words and actions of another person.

I cannot force Mark to play the guessing game. He'd run the risk of guessing wrong. So instead, I must offer a clear, direct statement, "I'm feeling lonely today; I wanted you to know."

We're also learning to ask questions rather than waiting for feelings to surface. When Mark says, "You seem restless today. What are you thinking?" I know that he has taken time to read my heart and wants to understand more.

When he says, "You really look tired. What can I do to lighten your load?" I know he wants to be a part of my solution.

We're learning to watch each other for clues. A deep sigh when he comes in the door and hangs his coat in the front hall closet tells me he's had a heavy day.

When Mark hears a high-pitched, high-speed chatter when we're in a crowd, he knows I'm feeling insecure. Looking over the crowd, he catches my attention and smiles or moves close to me and squeezes my hand. I know he understands. I am reassured.

We're learning that it's fun to spend an evening by ourselves doing nothing. A quiet strength comes from silent moments when we don't have to talk to anyone about anything.

When we do talk, we're learning it's okay to dream together about the future or reminisce about the past. These conversations become reminders of the grace of God in our marriage.

Are these moments wasted because I can't hold in my hand a finished product? Absolutely not. They are moments invested in oneness—a commodity money can't buy.

We're learning to establish rituals shared with no one but the two of us. That mystical union referred to in the wedding ceremony is enhanced by exclusiveness that stretches beyond the physical aspect of love.

During one stage of our marriage, hot peppermint tea and a doughnut on Wednesday nights at ten became a ritual. It was Mark's treat to me—served on a silver tray from our bedside table.

Praying together is becoming that kind of ritual for us. Our time of shared vulnerability before God. No one else hears. No one else knows. We lay aside our roles, our positions, our credentials.

Stripped bare of the trappings of life, we can approach God together as the people we are rather than as the people we'd like to be or the people others think we are.

Praying together is also an act of commitment; it shows Mark that his concerns are mine and vice versa. In a sense, sharing our concerns together with God establishes joint ownership. We are both strengthened and supported by the other's presence and participation in prayer.

Above all, we're discovering that intimacy breeds not dependency, but individual strength. Four days ago I kissed Mark good-by at TWA's Gate H3 and watched him leave on a service call for the body of Christ. The children and I drove home through rush-hour darkness, fixed ourselves a toast-and-scrambled-eggs dinner, and read books in bed until we fell asleep.

The other side of my bed was cold. All night I wondered where to put my feet. In the morning I smelled Mark's aftershave in the bathroom. His bottles were lined up neatly on his side of the medicine cabinet; his shirts were hanging limply in his side of the closet. All day I felt his presence, sensed the strength of his love, and waited for his call.

But life went on without Mark. The flu bug struck, a check bounced, a tire went flat on the way to church (along a busy two-lane highway with five children in the car), and a real-estate tax form didn't show up in time for our accountant. Monday morning the washer wouldn't start. Tuesday night a friend called to talk about her serious marriage problems.

Life's problems didn't wait for Mark to get back from his trip, so I did what needed to be done—at peace with myself and the world. For I knew that somewhere near Philadelphia was a man who would come home and say, "I love you, Honey. Tell me what I can do for you."

For the strength of intimacy, the joyful mystery of intimacy, is that when you lose your life to another person, you actually find it. Herein, it seems to me, is love at its highest.

Restoration

You can't smile at my sin,
It's not like you.
But still you smile at me.
You can't look me in the eyes
When I'm not looking at you,
  But you'll wait around
  And our eyes will meet again—
  My heart will say, "I'm sorry."
  Your look will say, "I'm sorry too."
  I'll feel your arm around me
  And we'll walk on.
  You and I.

Marathons and Purple Socks

When the alarm sounded at 5:30 A.M., the last thing I wanted to do was face a day of city traffic, a crowd of 10,000, and sixteen-mile-an-hour winds and driving rain.

I had said I'd go along to watch Mark run America's Marathon Chicago. But that was before I'd known what the weather conditions would be. Surely Mark, sensitive person that he was, would understand how much better off I'd be at home.

I pushed the snooze button and settled back for another two hours of luxurious warmth. After all, I thought, I'd had a nonstop week, the children needed my time, and weekends were for refueling.

By the time I got to the end of my excuses, I was wide awake. Going into the city with Mark must have been a bigger commitment than I'd thought; why else would I be feeling so guilty about two more hours of sleep? My feet hit the floor. I knew I had to go.

So it was that I found myself under four layers of rainproof gear, frantically clutching my umbrella lest the stiff Chicago wind carry it away, watching from the sidelines as 10,000 runners took on twenty-six miles of streets. Mark's number was 6,942. From an umbrella behind me, rain dripped down my back, and my fingers, numb with cold, struggled to pour another cup of coffee from my thermos.

Four hours and who knows how many city blocks later, I pressed against the damp mass of humanity that crowded near the finish line. Knowing Mark would come into sight momentarily, I stood even with the giant clock above the finish line.

The rain had stopped, but the wetness had already caused the dye from my loafers to turn my gray socks purple. The banana bread and coffee I'd brought were long gone. But Mark was heading for the finish line. He had conquered.

As I wrapped a warm, dry blanket around him, offering my shoulder for him to lean on as we made our way to the car, I had a sudden sense of what support in marriage is all about.

"You know, today you gave me one of the most meaningful gifts you've ever given me," Mark said that evening as we sat in our warm family room and nursed his sore feet.

Until that moment I'd had no idea how much my support had meant to him. And then I remembered that love isn't love until it goes out of its way for another. With Christ and the Cross as my example, I'm amazed how quickly I forget the truth.

CHAPTER FOUR

The Mystery
of Letting Go

Sometimes It Rains on Our Parade

Homecoming is supposed to be colored leaves, crisp sunshine, blue skies. Instead, we awoke to wet weather that promised to batter the area for twelve hours.

"Mother," Jori wailed as she bounded into the kitchen. "It's raining on our floats! And my first homecoming too."

The gloom did not lighten as we drove bravely toward the high school. Crisp fall was reduced to sog and saturation; the heavens came toward us in sheets.

But as we turned onto Prince Crossing Road, the dust flew. Just beyond the next hill sprawled a *dry* football field.

"See," Jori pronounced with glee, "the Lord knows where Wheaton Christian High is."

I felt a Bible verse coming—the one about the rain

that falls on the righteous and the unrighteous. Somewhere in the world rain was falling on someone's float, even if homecoming was sponsored by Christians. Age fourteen was not too early for her to learn life's realities, I thought.

But the sermon would have to wait. Jori headed for the sidelines as soon as I pulled into the parking lot.

Later, as we dumped the remnants of homecoming on the kitchen table after a nearly perfect day, the phone rang.

"Mom. It's for you."

That night I didn't recite my Scripture verse to Jori. Instead I sat by her bed and eased her into the painful reality of the phone call.

The diagnosis on Beth, her good friend and Bible study partner, had been confirmed by a third neurosurgeon: inoperable brain tumor.

Jori disappeared under the pillows of her bed, unable to talk. When at last she found her spirit again, she said simply, "I knew it, Mom. I knew it was something awful."

As I kissed her good-night I realized I still had not recited the verse to her: "He . . . sends rain on the righteous and the unrighteous" (Matthew 5:45).

Jori was learning its message without her mother's sermon.

Letting Go

 Few places have I felt motherhood more painfully than at Midway Airport gate B3, a place of coming and going. I have waved good-by on the departure ramp and hugged hello on arrivals. But today is different. The sensation feels somewhat like having a tooth pulled— yanked from the roots that bury it deep. Today a part of me is being yanked away.

Eleven-year-old Nick looks impeccable in his new gray-and-blue spring jacket. A piece of his blond hair sticks straight up in back even though we tried to slick it down with hair spray. He hands the agent his ticket to Philadelphia as though he is buying candy at the corner store. He grins the grin of self-satisfaction.

"You're not scared, are you, Mom?" he asks, tucking his boarding pass into his jacket pocket just as I'd instructed him earlier.

"No Nick, I'm not scared. Just a little sentimental I guess. Mothers are that way, you know."

He grins as though he knows, but I know he cannot possibly know. He cannot sense that emotional umbilical cord that keeps me wanting to be his support system long after he's escaped the womb. How could he know how hard it is for a mother to begin releasing her child? He gives my arm a little squeeze just the same.

I hear the boarding call on the intercom and hold him tight for a brief moment. Then he is gone. He turns and waves before disappearing down the ramp. I watch window seven. As the Midway Metrolink turns east, I see the dim outline of a face, then a fisted hand with a thumb pointing upward. "All's in control, Mom," it says.

He's growing up—a frightening reality for a mother. I stand and watch as the silver bird shrinks to a dot in the blue. I can do nothing more for my son. The thought strikes an uneasy chord somewhere down deep and begins my pangs of severance. I knew they would come sooner or later, but I am not ready just yet. Metrolink Airliners don't wait around until mothers feel ready, though. They take off on schedule. I sense that is what is happening to my son.

I walk through corridors filled with a blur of people. I think of another mother who had to give up her son, not to a DC-9 bound for Philadelphia but to a reed basket on the river Nile; not for a week of spring vacation, but for eternity. My risk is nothing compared to the one faced by the mother of Moses, but I struggle just the same. Whether the destination is Philadelphia or Pharaoh's house, giving up is hard to do.

I turn the empty car toward home, comforted by the thought that sometimes it is in the unnatural act—the act of surrender—that we keep the most. The pangs of letting go will continue; there is no turning back. But down deep I know that both Nick and I will be stronger for it.

Birds Have to Fly

I watch the storm move in from the southwest and listen to the tornado warnings on the radio. Dark cloud masses roll across the horizon. I go through the house closing the windows and thinking how glad I am everyone is home. Then I notice the robins, perched precariously on a middle branch of our backyard crab apple tree. Mother and two babies.

"She's not going to make them fly into this storm," I say to myself as I watch the drama unfold. The crab apple tree jerks as if it were tied to the wind by an invisible string. Mother and babies jerk with it. The babies flap their wings and almost lose balance. Their heads are still wet and wobbly—much too immature for these near-tornado winds.

But I am a mother of a different kind. I do not know what is right for robins. Still, I think it is a big mistake to teach your babies to fly when the winds are so turbulent. I wonder if she might not come to her senses and tuck them safely back into their nest where they belong. But when I come back, several hours later, both branch and nest are empty. The winds are still restless, but no baby robins lie smashed against the ground.

"Can you think of a better way to strengthen their wings?" Mark asks later when I tell him my fears for the robins.

I've never liked strong winds—not as a child when hurricane winds pounded the gulf coast near our home, nor today as an adult when tornadoes stalk the Midwest. Sometimes I struggle just as much with winds of a different kind. Often the mother in me wants to walk through my children's lives and close windows against the storms outside. I would not have them fly into turbulence.

But today, storm or not outside, it's time for me, like Mother Robin, to let my offspring fly. Jori has turned sixteen. I hand her the keys to the car and watch from the front porch as she drives away into the rain. Alone. We are no longer going with her. She toots the horn and waves good-by in exuberance.

I think also of another storm. When Jesus walked on the water toward his disciples, the Peter that climbed out of the boat to meet him was a child. The Peter that returned, though dripping wet, was a man who could proclaim with confidence, "Truly you are the Son of God" (Matthew 14:33). In the storms we often learn the most. I must trust my child to the storms.

The wind is still restless and the robin's nest still empty. The hands on the mantle clock crawl slowly through the evening. I pick up the newspaper to read, but mostly to wait for ten when Jori will return. We can never go back, Jori and I. When the time comes, robins must fly, storm or not. "What better way to strengthen their wings," Mark had said. I know he is right.

Horse Thief Lake

We almost miss Horse Thief Lake as we drive on Highway 244 just west of Mt. Rushmore. Road construction takes us off the beaten path, the afternoon sun is low in the sky, and complaints are coming from the back seat. "We're hungry. Aren't we almost there?"

I'm not sure where "there" is. Just a clean campsite somewhere under the towering pines will do. As the road curves the children spot the lake and proclaim in unison, "There's a lake. Let's stop here."

I'm not at all taken with their idea. We need a campsite, not a lake. This place isn't even listed in our guide. Probably a crummy spot. Reason enough to keep moving. Besides, we have no time for swimming. My mind rehearses our evening routine. Set up tent. Pump air mattresses. Light the stove. Haul water. Cook dinner. Everyone has a job to do before we play.

But we turn down the dirt road and weave around the lake. Hidden in a far corner we find an empty space— towering pines, lake view, and all. I see the high granite walls at the north end of the lake. Tiny figures move at the top, then hurl themselves through the air. A faraway splash, shrieks of delight, and my worst fears are confirmed. This is not an ordinary mountain lake nestled high in the Black Hills. This is a "jump-from-the-high-rocks" type of mountain lake.

"Be careful on those rocks," I call after the children as they set out to explore the lake. They are back in a flash. "Please, can't we go swimming? We promise we'll do our jobs later. It looks so cool." I think of the long, hot hours in the van. Mark and I agree to the swim, and they are gone. I look toward the rocks. They only asked to swim. Surely, they won't jump off the rocks.

I volunteer for campsite duty while Daddy takes waterfront. Later, camp in order and dinner started, I head toward the lake to see about my swimmers. As I turn a bend in the path, I spot Nick poised on a ledge thirty feet in the air, ready to plunge into Horse Thief Lake. His daddy and sister are close behind.

I want to scream, to rush up those rocks and snatch my eleven-year-old to safety. He spies me on the path below and yells, "It's okay, Mom. Watch me jump."

Don't, Nick. But the words stay in my throat. I close my eyes in agony until I hear the splash.

"See me, Mom?" he yells after bobbing to the surface. He looks as though he has just conquered Mt. Everest.

Later, around the campfire, he talks with great pride of his exploits of the day. Next morning we break camp, head west, and I assume Horse Thief Lake is just another of life's inconsequential moments.

Several years later, when Nick was walking the peaks

and valleys of junior-high years, he asked me one day, "Know when I felt real close to God, Mom? When I was up on those rocks, about to jump into Horse Thief Lake."

I give him a big hug. *Thank you, Lord, that I didn't say "Don't."*

The significance of that moment high above Horse Thief Lake sobers me. Any moment. Every moment. All are redeemable for God in the life of my children, if only I let go.

Dear Jori

I stand by your bed and watch you sleep—innocent, peaceful, oblivious. A few blocks away another mother's child sleeps, in a different kind of peace. I know I must break the news. I stand outside your door and cry. Soon I will stand beside you and cry. Beth was your friend.

I wonder what I will say to you. Will we talk about the time in junior high when the two of you illustrated the entire book of James for your after-school Bible study? You drew rainbows over the bottom of the page about trials. Only the two of you knew what they meant. Maybe we will talk about your favorite song—the one you and Beth requested every Friday night on our local Christian radio station. "A Friend's a Friend Forever . . ." Maybe you will pull out the poem entitled "What Is a Friend?"—the one you wrote to Beth when you were in eighth grade. I look at the picture on your dresser of the Beth we knew before the brain tumor. The white porcelain frame with hearts around it was Beth's gift to you on your thirteenth birthday. Maybe we will talk about that birthday party. It would do you good, I think.

"She's in heaven now." I am startled by my own words. Your eyes open wide as though you've been waiting. "Beth" is all you say. I nod. You turn your face to the wall and cover your head with your pillow. "Mother, please, I need to be alone."

I close the door on your grief. The hurt burns in my throat—the hurt of your loss and the hurt of my helplessness. I want to take you on my lap and hold you close, the way I did when you were three and stubbed your toe. But you are almost sixteen now. You choose to grieve alone, at least for now. I listen to your muffled sobs. I take a new box of Kleenex to you. I sense I am still the intruder so I leave again.

Later I stand by you at the funeral home as you thumb through Beth's scrapbook. Together we look at her pictures and remember your happy times together—a concert, Great America, a slumber party. Your poem is there, printed in your neat handwriting and signed, "Your friend forever, Jori." I sit by you during the funeral. We hand each other Kleenex as we listen to the pastor read the poem you wrote to Beth. Someone sings, "A Friend's a Friend Forever," and I reach out and squeeze your hand.

I must be able to do something more. I am your mother. But today I cannot. As we follow the long gray hearse, I wonder if the greatest gift I can give you in your pain is the freedom to grieve in your own way, even when you choose to grieve alone.

Where Has All the Laughter Gone?

Laughter doesn't live here anymore.
It went away with the phone call.
Tonight ours is a house of tears;
A broken heart
Unquieted love

I feel her ache
Like a soft pincushion full of pricks.
Why should reality have to start
When you're fourteen?
Only fourteen.
Too early to
Put away childish things.
I am forty,
But we cry together.
Hard cruel world

That metes out pain on the innocent young.
What does it mean to say "I love you"
And the next day change your mind?

I watch her as she packs up her heart
And prepares to give it back.
A black-and-orange football jersey.
She wore it everywhere,
Even to bed.
A stuffed kitty
(Her first significant gift)
That bore his name,
Only spelled backward
So it was not quite so obvious.
A happy moment caught between a gold picture frame.
The two of them leaning against a tree at summer camp.

Where has all my laughter gone?
Packed in a box with a shattered teenage love.
I grieve for her disappointment today;
I sorrow for all her disappointments tomorrow.
And the tears from her hurt
Etch themselves around my heart
Like icicles on a frozen day—
They don't go away.

I feel the lines of age;
The stripping away of my carefreeness.
Rachel weeping for her children.
By the rivers of Babylon we sat and wept
When we remembered Zion.
"Sing us the songs of Zion."

But my children's pain inspires no song.
Responsibility for them weighs on my spirit,
And the shower I get from a water balloon
Is no longer a joke.
Playfulness exchanged for a sermon
On how to be considerate of adults.
Whatever happened to fun?
Remember when water balloons were jubilation
And cartoons from the newspaper were celebrations?
Remember when jokes were funny?
Three cheers for life

And you and your children went down
With a last hurrah.

I walked among laughter once
And I remember:
A dad,
Three-piece suit and all,
Kneeling on the floor of Kay-Bee Toys

Zipping a race car
Bright red and yellow
Through plastic loop-de-loops.
Father and son
Caught together in
Loops of plastic play.
A time to laugh.
I hear their joy
Even as I walk on through the mall.

I remember laughter
In the middle of a Jewel parking lot.
Mother and daughter
In a contest of shopping carts.
"Beat you to the car!"
Milk cartons bouncing
Eggs rattling
But mother won the race.
A time to laugh.
And I feel the joy all the way home.

Lord, bring back the captives to Zion
Refill our mouths with laughter
Even when we must weep with our children.

Smiles, Miles, and Happy Moms

"Smile, Mom! You look much better when you do."

Nick's words startle me. I haven't been told to smile since I was a kid in Sunday school and we sang, "If you have a little frown, turn it upside down. Everyone ought to keep smiling."

Obligingly, I flex my face, then close the front door and head toward Klein Creek for my daily two-mile hike. The late-afternoon sun is mellow, the park tranquil. But I cannot forget Nick's words. I cross the wooden bridge and wonder what prompted his admonition.

I consider myself a pleasant person. No dark shadows have followed me through life. Most of my childhood and adult years have been more like sunny picnics. I've known moments of pain—some private, some not so private. But on the whole, my life has brought more smiling than crying.

On the other hand, I have never been one to manufacture smiles just to make myself look better—or to make someone else feel better. If I've had a long day and my head aches, I don't rehearse smiles before my family comes to the dinner table. I think of myself as much too "authentic" for that. And I've always had trouble smiling into a camera. I avoid staged smiling whenever possible.

What, then, do I do with Nick's words? Disregard them as mere child's chatter or assume some serious deficiency in our relationship? What kind of a mother am I that my son has to beg for a smile? I decide that neither extreme is valid, but I will not ignore Nick's comment.

Long ago I came to the conclusion that it is wise to listen carefully to those who know me best. They give me the stripped-down version of who I really am. "Think about how you're coming across" is a line we use often with our children. I'd never thought to apply it to myself. *How am I coming across?* I wonder today as I pass the first clump of cottonwood along the creek.

Home is where you can be yourself—an oasis of authenticity. If I don't feel like smiling, why smile? The people who love me will keep on loving me whether I smile or not. It is part of the magic we call home and family and love—no conditions attached.

I turn west into the park. My favorite mallard sits in the middle of the lagoon, surrounded by sunset on water. I cannot miss the analogy of this peaceful scene. Why smile for my family? A genuine smile is a scene of peace. It reflects what is going on inside me even as the lagoon reflects the western sky.

What is in my heart eventually appears on my face. Jesus used different words to make the same point when he said, "The good man brings good things out of the good stored up in him" (Matthew 12:35).

I suspect that all too often the ones I love see deep lines of weariness, worry, and responsibility etched on my face—everything but peace. If a twelve-year-old could analyze his words, Nick would probably agree that he was asking not so much for a smile as for a happy mom.

A popular phrase says "Smile, God loves you." Although God's love is valid motivation for smiling, I believe God, like Nicky, is more concerned with my attitude than with my smiles. There will be days I don't smile even though I know God loves me. When I am without a smile, my family will have to take my word that I love them. But if anyone deserves my smiles, it is my family. If there is any place I should reflect happiness, it is at home.

I make the final loop toward home and cross Klein Creek for the second time. I am hot, my feet are tired, and a biker almost runs me off the path. As I drop onto our front porch swing, I catch a glimpse of myself in the window. Nick was right. I do look better when I smile.

The Bike That Talked About God

Maybe God knew my bike was getting to be more important to me than God," Nick reflects as we sit on the front porch swing waiting for his ride to school. He is still struggling with the reality that his cherished bike, the one he built with his own hands, is gone—stolen from its usual spot in the garage. Two days after opening the garage door and finding it missing, he is still in shock.

"Why would anyone want to steal my bike? A whole year of building and saving . . ." He brightens momentarily and laughs over the many nights he slept with half a bike next to his bed. The day he rode the finished project down the driveway for the first time, we all stood and cheered.

Why do things and people we love sometimes disappear from our lives? It is a question as deep as the pain. I don't even try to answer it. I simply say, "Nick, your bike was stolen because someone wanted what you had. Today, God puts his arms around you and says, 'Okay, Nick, the bike is gone. Now, what can you and I learn through it?'"

Nick is quiet for a moment longer. Then he stands, hugs me, and is off to school. I know he is learning, not only about an evil world but also about a loving God.

The Sacrifice

No one said much at dinner. The empty chair said it all. The preacher cleared his throat and reached for his Bible. His eyes paused on the empty plate. His daughter never came.

The preacher smiled weakly at his wife. He wished he could say, "It will be all right." But he didn't know.

As usual, he read from the Bible. But his words sounded hollow. His mind took him far away. How far, he didn't know. His mind was with his daughter, wherever she was. His prayer faltered.

Where had he failed? His mind raced over the past fifteen years of his ministry. Life had not always been easy, but it had been good.

He and his wife, with her seemingly endless resources of quiet strength, were proud of their four boys and one girl. Their children were typical. Rambunctious. Fun. Intensely loyal to one another.

There had been storms at the preacher's house, but nothing that caused serious damage. He chalked them up to experience. But then the wind shifted. The preacher watched and prayed. When he saw the storm coming, he began battening down the hatches.

People across the hollows and the cotton fields of southern Alabama knew the preacher. For twelve years he had comforted them, steadied drunken feet, and pushed stranded travelers out of ditches. He had driven miles to take them to the nearest hospital in the middle of the night and had sat by the fire of one who earlier had pointed a gun at him. Yes, the preacher was always there.

People knew he would stop by to sit on their porch and talk. They knew he would hammer nails with them, bring them a load of firewood from his woods, come by with his car to take them to church. They knew he would marry them, bury them, and sit with them when they were sick.

They knew about the little churches he built. They gave him land and worked side by side with him. They came to hear him preach. They lined the crude wooden benches or sat on folding chairs under a tent. Many changed their life's direction as a result of his preaching. They grew strong. And when the time came for the preacher to reach out to the people thirty miles up the road, they cried and waved good-by but continued the love he had begun.

The preacher was a family man. When he helped deliver calves, he took his children. When he sat all night with a grieving family, one of his five sat with him. When he went to the jails, a small one went along. His children sat around fireplaces with him when he taught the Bible to neighbors. They sat on porches with him, hammered nails with him, made emergency hospital trips with him, gathered firewood with him, and heard him marry, bury, preach, and pray.

Now his children were growing up. Almost overnight, his daughter became a strange mixture of child and adult, calm and fury, delight and despair, laughter and tears, stubbornness and tenderness. The preacher loved her. He understood the passage to adulthood. He sensed her passage would be rockier than most, but he hoped to steer her around the boulders.

The preacher had based his values on Scripture. He hoped his children would do the same. But his daughter had friends with different values, and their values were beginning to overshadow his. Honesty, openness, truthfulness, respect, self-discipline, hard work, prayer, and obedience were becoming less important to his daughter.

The preacher hurt deeply.

At first came innocent spend-the-night parties with girlfriends. Then came scrawled notes sent home with her brother. "Dad, I'll be late getting home from school. I have to stay and help on a project. A friend will bring me home."

Then came flimsy excuses about why she didn't get home from her nine-to-five Saturday job at Elmore's Variety store until eleven and the hasty exits after Sunday dinner to go for a ride with older girlfriends. She never mentioned where their three-hour drives took them.

Porch lights stayed on and dinners got cold while the preacher and his wife waited and wondered.

They thought about their life of service to the Lord, of

the three little churches they had helped build, and of the hundreds of people who needed them.

There had been tests, but they had passed. There had been discouragement, but comfort had come. There had been sacrifices, but they had not cost them their family.

They also thought of their daughter. Though they gained Escambia and Conecuh County, they could lose their own daughter. Would it be worth it?

They thought of their future. Every year, more and more people said, "Move up here. Start a church for us too." They saw their future in little communities without churches.

They also thought of their daughter's future. Could they expect to grow a healthy plant if they ignored nature's havoc on the tender sprout? As good farmers, they knew that a young plant having trouble needed a more suitable place to grow.

Their decision tore them from the people they loved. From their land and their home. From the ministry into which they had poured their life's blood. It left gaping holes. Who would shoulder the burdens? Who would love as they had loved?

But who could love their daughter as they could? Who could share her needs as they could? No sacrifice was too great. The transplant took place.

The East had churches with large youth groups, seminary-educated staffs, trained visitation groups, and Christian psychologists. No one needed the preacher, his firewood, his steady hand, or his car. Wood sold for thirty dollars a cord, retreat centers treated alcoholics, and emergency ambulance service came within three minutes to carry the sick to the hospital.

For a while, the preacher drove a bread truck and sold

meat to feed his family. It was perhaps his greatest ministry. His young flower blossomed.

The preacher lost his church. But he saved his daughter. I know. The preacher was my father.

CHAPTER FIVE

The Mystery
of Time

Look to the Rock

Most people can drive through Range, Alabama, and never know they've been there. But not if you are the preacher's daughter, coming home after twenty-five years. Highway 47 follows the old railroad line, then makes a 45-degree turn at Jackson's store. Just beyond the bend in the road is the white clapboard schoolhouse, once flour mill, now community center. The road curves through Miles Jackson's pasture, skirts Noah Bell's cotton field, and ends, for me, at the white cement block church with a tiny square porch on the front and two Sunday school rooms at the rear.

Tonight, twenty-five years have no meaning. I am fifteen again and the preacher's daughter. I slide onto the pine bench and take a red paperback songbook from the rack in front of me. Cardboard fans on wooden sticks still remind me of funeral homes and doctor's tongue depressors. We sing "There's a land that is fairer than day. And by faith we shall see it afar . . . In the sweet, bye and bye . . ."

I study the picture on the wall—the one of a little girl walking across a bridge at night with an angel hovering nearby. It hangs just above the gas heater, near where we huddled when the temperature dropped. The attendance board says 43 for last Sunday, and $35.60 for the offering.

I look at the faithful faces around me: Clevie, my bus driver, who still says "Yes ma'am" and "no sir" to everyone; Manse Edwards, who took us fishing in his boat and riding in his green pickup truck; Doris Bell, who made us buttermilk biscuits; Iverlee Jackson, who brought us our mail and delivered telephone messages because his store had the only phone for miles around; and Erma Ruth McCall, who my daddy led to Christ before the little church was even built.

Clara Pettus smiles at me from the third row and afterward gets tears in her eyes as she recalls the night my daddy sat all night with her family when her husband died. "It was 1955, April third," she says with the sound of sorrow. I notice how young she looks for 87.

Daddy walks to the pulpit as though he's never been away. His voice spans the years and pulls us back to the community we once were. I am suddenly aware that I have never left this place or these people. I have taken them with me. They are as much a part of me as my dark eyes and brown hair. I think of the prophet Isaiah who once reminded his people to "Look to the rock from which you were cut and to the quarry from which you were hewn" (Isaiah 51:1).

I must return to Jackson's store and the old flour mill to help me understand who I am today. I must stop at the little white concrete church at the bend in the road to remember my commitments to God. I am bound forever to Range, Alabama, and to Conecuh County Highway 47. Retracing my steps tells me how much.

Music From the
Grand Chickering

The Chickering grand piano looked as if it belonged on red velvet carpet in the drawing room of an antebellum mansion. Instead, it sat on gray concrete, squeezed between hand-hewn benches and a plain pine pulpit, in a little country church in Range, Alabama. Even against cement-block walls, the piano's rosewood casing and its intricately carved legs looked regal. As a nine-year-old, I fantasized about where the piano might have been. The governor's mansion in Montgomery? A plantation in Huntsville? The estate of a timber baron in Brewton? But its origins were not nearly as important as the role it played in a parent-child relationship.

The donor of the grand piano was a mystery. Someone had heard about Daddy's church and had written to ask if the preacher would like a piano. One day a truck arrived, backed up to the front entrance of the church, and unloaded the majestic Chickering. My mother, the church pianist, was especially pleased. The piano was a work of art, almost too fine to touch. I squatted and studied the delicate designs of the leg carvings; I looked at my image in the gleaming rosewood casing. I had never seen anything so fine. Daddy propped the lid open, and Mother said, "Well, Ruth Ann, aren't you going to play it?"

Me, play a piano that looked as if it belonged to court musicians? I was barely out of *John Thompson,* book three. But I took my place on the piano stool after Daddy adjusted it to fit my height. "The Spinning Song" sounded like an organ concerto. I closed my eyes and imagined a big cathedral in Europe.

Daddy assigned me the care of the piano. Every Saturday afternoon when my brothers and I cleaned the church, I went straight for the piano. I waxed and polished the mahogany until my brothers teased that I would surely wipe the casing away. On Sunday mornings before church, I opened the heavy wooden lid. After church I put the lid down.

After school each day, I walked across the yard, music books in hand, opened the church door, and sat down at the Chickering to practice. From my place on the piano stool, I could look out the window, trace clouds in the sky, or watch birds flutter over the bean patch. There I enjoyed a quiet kind of solace—the gentle music, the clouds, the birds, the bean patch, the piano, and me.

One Sunday morning several years later, Daddy said, "Ruth Ann, how would you like to play the piano for Sunday school some morning? You choose the songs you'd like us to sing, practice them, and let me know when you're ready." At first I thought he was being his usual tease, but his face was serious. He really *did* want me for his accompanist.

I doubled my practice time. I started at the beginning and went page by page through every song in the red paperback *Gospel Songbook*. Mrs. Bushbee, my piano teacher at school, sent a note home that said, "Ruth Ann is making unusual progress in her music. Keep encouraging her."

One day I announced proudly to Daddy that I'd like us to sing "What a Friend We Have in Jesus" and "For God So Loved the World." The next Sunday when Daddy announced the songs, I took my place at the piano. My hands shook so badly I could hardly feel the keys, and I used the soft pedal for the entire song. I forgot a B-flat or two and played the wrong measure for an introduction, but Daddy thanked me politely when we finished singing, and after church Mother came to hug me and say how proud she was.

I wish I could say that I went on to become a concert pianist or an accomplished musician. Today I'm neither. But I did become our Sunday school pianist, and when Mother took time off to have another baby I filled in for her during worship services. I played the simple gospel hymns with little flourish but with great feeling and pride. It didn't matter that I would never be a famous pianist. Mother and Daddy believed in me. They made me their Sunday school pianist even though an adult could probably have done it better.

Trusting your child is a theme as old as the story of Moses. In order to save her son's life, Moses's mother placed him in a waterproof basket among the reeds along the Nile River and left her daughter Miriam to watch over her baby brother. With a mother's statement of trust like that, it is little wonder that Miriam went on to become a great leader of her people. A parent's trust is a powerful motivator, whether it be watching over a basket in the Nile River or playing "For God So Loved the World" for Sunday school.

The antique Chickering piano no longer sits at the front of the little church in Range, Alabama. A smaller upright has taken its place. But in my mind I carry the image of that grand piano, and I remember what it felt like to have parents who trusted me enough to let me share their ministry. No wonder ministry is such a happy thought for me today.

With You Always

I am alone, wrapped in angry, atmospheric gray. The wide-bodied DC-10 vibrates with the wrath of the storm. For all emotional purposes, I am alone—just me and a planeful of meaningless others.

But I sense another. Moments earlier we had walked together to the end of the concourse. We have taken a lifetime of walks together.

The two of us walked together when the night gobbled up little girls and the path through the woods to a friend's house moved through mysterious shadows, when thunder shook the house and lightning pointed ugly spears in our direction, when hurricane gales whipped in from the coast, and when guns in the night shot bullets into the house down the road and drunks knocked on our door at two o'clock in the morning.

"Even though I walk through the valley of the shadow

of death, I will fear no evil, for you are with me" (Psalm 23:4).

We had sat together at the airport gate, sometimes talking, sometimes not. But nothing was more important than sitting and waiting together. We have done a lifetime of sitting together. When the fish were biting at Manse Edward's lake, father and child sat in silence, bound together by a fishing boat and time. When a brown cocker spaniel died, father and child sat together and cried on an old log near the pecan tree that marked the grave.

"Even though I walk through the valley of the shadow of death, I will fear no evil, for you are with me" (Psalm 23:4).

When we parted at the boarding gate, moisture gathered in his eyes. "It's not an easy time," he said. "But life goes on . . . and God is with us."

With us. With me. With you always. In flesh and blood I saw the meaning. For another Father had walked with me through the shadows, grieved with me over loss, sat with me while I waited, flown with me through the storms.

I had seen God's love in the flesh of a father who was not just *for* me—but always *with* me.

The Gift That Never Changed

It is a simple, red, leather-bound Bible. But to me it is much more than words in leather wrapping. Today it links my past and present. It has been a part of every transition. Today, it calls me to remember . . .

An early morning sunrise. I am eight years old. Seldom do I get up this early, but today I am on my way to camp. Anticipation keeps me from sleep. My suitcase, packed and ready, sits waiting at the end of my bed. I tiptoe through the pre-dawn house. I wonder, *will everything be the same when I get back? Will my dog Susie still know me? Will mother still remind me to put my sweater on and please not to crack my gum so loudly?*

I find mother on the front porch swing with her red leather Bible open in her lap. I sit beside her, and she talks to God about camp and about me. I am less afraid.

A rainy night in August. I am eighteen years old. The same blue suitcase sits packed and waiting at the end of my bed. This time a trunk and an assortment of boxes and bags are stacked nearby. I look around the little room— the one corner of the world I'd called my own. *Will it still be mine after a semester of college? Will mother still come and sit on the edge of my bed and talk after I come home from an evening out? Will my brothers still borrow my radio and eavesdrop on my phone conversations? Will my Manheim Central High School pennants still be hanging on the wall?*

I go toward my parents' room to say one last good night. Mother is kneeling by her bed, her red leather Bible open before her. I kneel beside her as she talks to God about college and about me. I am reassured.

A house full of wedding guests. I am twenty-one years old. Cars with out-of-town license plates line the circular driveway that leads to the front porch. I wait for the clock to run its cycle. This time tomorrow night, I will be Mark's wife. The thought has a certain mystery about it—like trying to imagine what life on the moon would be like. I do not know whether to laugh or cry.

I walk through the silent space that has been my home. The long wide hallway houses the family photo gallery. I look at myself as a nine-month-old and wonder what my own daughter will look like someday. I wonder what will change now that I am leaving home for good. *Will Daddy still give me bear hugs and call me his little girl? Will Mother still ask if I need a sweater? Will she still bake my favorite treat—Moravian Sugar Cake—when I come home?*

I walk past the living room. Mother is sitting in her favorite chair, her red leather Bible open in front of her. I sit beside her. With wedding gifts piled high all around us, Mother, as though giving me one last gift, talks to God about my marriage and about me. I am ready for the unknown.

I don't see many red leather Bibles anymore, and I don't kneel much to pray. Most of my prayers are on the run, not on my knees. But today I pick up Mother's red leather Bible and wonder what more valuable gift I could leave my children than lasting memories of a mother who read her Bible and prayed for her children.

When the Moon Doesn't Shine

Usually the moon shines bright on clear May nights in eastern Pennsylvania. But tonight the moon is missing. All is dark. I notice brown circles under the lamp in the hall when mother welcomes our 2:00 A.M. arrival from Illinois. I also notice brown circles under her eyes. Spots I'd never noticed before. Tired skin under gentle folds.

But here she stands, my mother for forty years. I sense an accumulation of nights waiting up for home-coming children, as though the years have cast shadows from the lamp onto her face. I see the years in the black and blue veins that have just this week felt the heart specialist's probe. I hear the years—like the ocean ringing in a seashell—in the doctor's diagnosis. "Red flag . . . enlarged heart . . . slow the pace . . ." I stare into uncertainty.

Mother has been a steady pulse through the years. Tomorrow has been an assumed promise—a grand procession of family weddings, births, graduations, music recitals, ordinations, Christmas, Easter, Thanksgiving. Time has been an event, not a sequence.

As I look at Mother, I sense that someone has wound the clock. Time now has a cadence. Years have become increments. History has a beginning and an end. I shiver in the early morning chill. But then Mother's arms wrap me in warmth, and I am home. A forty-year-old child reassured by her mother's touch. There is no time in touch. Welcoming arms know not the years.

I hear the tea kettle whistling. Freshly baked chocolate chip cookies wait on the old ironstone plate that once served cookies from Grandma Hollinger's kitchen. Mother's chocolate chip cookies and Grandma Hollinger's ironstone plate pull me back into timelessness. We sip peppermint tea and laugh over a silly story Daddy tells. Our laughter drowns out the clock. There is no time in laughter. Mother laughs the hardest of all. Dark circles. Tired circles of joy. Her children are home.

For a moment I forget bruised veins and ticking clocks. I am held together by things that do not change— a mother's early morning welcome, freshly baked chocolate chip cookies, an ironstone plate, peppermint tea, a mantel clock, and laughter. I am held together by a God who does not change. I know the God of time who is yet above time. I see tonight in my mother's face the strange paradox of time and timelessness. A rare glimpse of the divine.

Maybe Next Year

You're not coming home for Christmas?" Mother's gentle voice on the other end of the line conveys a trace of hurt. She struggles to recover.

"It just won't be the same," she says. "I know eight hundred miles is a terribly long drive, especially with the cost of gas these days. And we did just see you in September. But it will be different, not having you here to celebrate."

Her voice regains its strength.

"Well, we can send the presents United Parcel and call you Christmas day," she says. "And this way the children won't have to miss their Sunday school program."

I am relieved that she sees it my way. Mark and I are sure we have made the right decision.

Now that Nick and Jori are getting older, spending the holidays with their friends has become more important. They don't enjoy being cramped up in the back seat of a car for fifteen hours one way while their friends toboggan in freedom down snowy slopes.

"Nobody else goes to his grandma's house *every* Christmas. We miss out on all the fun around here."

"There's nothing to do there except play Parcheesi and talk about the old days. Can't we stay home? Just this once?"

They are right. It is time we start our own Christmas traditions. Who says every Christmas celebration has to have a twenty-four-pound turkey and sixteen people around the dining table?

What about a dinner for four in the peace and tranquility of our own home? I will prepare my own recipes and serve food on Christmas dishes I've never had a chance to use.

We will enjoy opening presents, just the four of us, on Christmas morning. For once we won't have to rush through the evening gift exchange on December 20 to get ready to leave the next day on that long drive to Grandpa's house.

I won't have to sit Indian style in the car, my legs tucked underneath me to avoid a foot encounter with the thermos, picnic basket, books, and game bag.

We won't have to feed dollar bills to greedy toll booths, tolerate salt trucks that spit chemicals all over our windshield, or endure grumpy children who argue and complain in the back seat.

"When are we gonna get there? Daddy, he's on *my* side. Yes, he is! His foot is over the hump."

"There's nothing to do. I already read all my books. You mean we have seven more hours to go?"

"My tummy hurts. I think I'm gonna throw up."

Tonight I am far from childish chatter, hungry toll booths, and a cramped front seat. Jori has just lit the last candle on our Advent wreath. And Nicky, garbed in bathrobe and towel, is reading a story about the little shepherd boy.

A smooth order eases us through the evening. I'm glad we are home, just the four of us together on Christmas Eve. I have nothing to do but sit back, relax, and reflect upon the mystery of the God-Child.

But the evening has a strange ambivalence. The oak log spits its red-hot embers against the fireplace screen, and something sad burns in the sparks. The glowing log ejects a part of its core, the fiber that made it oak.

What about my family, my extended family? Having Christmas for four certainly doesn't mean we have permanently rejected grandparents, aunts, uncles, cousins.

I try to convince myself, but I feel disconnected from my old home, as if I've forgotten a part of Christmas.

For the third time, I turn the stack of Christmas records and sweep together the scattered popcorn kernels.

The children spread their sleeping bags in front of the blazing hearth—a new family tradition Jori has suggested.

Grandma's house has no fireplace. The children hang their stockings along the staircase banister. After all the little cousins are tucked safely in bed, Grandpa fills the stockings.

I move my rocker closer to the roaring fire and watch as the once solid log crumbles into ashes. From somewhere in the night, I hear muffled sounds of carolers coming closer.

"We wish you a merry Christmas, we wish you a merry Christmas . . ."

Peering from the front windows, we see a group of

neighbors lined along our driveway. Their carols draw me back to past Christmases.

Caroling on Christmas Eve was our family tradition. We'd sing and then give out baskets of Mother's sandtarts and holiday spritz to some of the older folks in the neighborhood. They always looked forward to our visits. Some told Mom and Dad that they almost cried when they saw us coming.

"You don't see many families like yours anymore— having fun and doing things together. Everybody's too busy. Keep bringing those children by to see us, even if there are sixteen of you. We love to see 'em all."

So Daddy promised he would.

I knew he felt proud to have all of us there, singing together, throwing snowballs at each other, racing down the streets, and sliding on the firmly packed snow—just as we'd done when we were kids.

By the time we had delivered the last basket, our voices would be cracking with cold on the high notes of "Joy to the World." We'd trudge back up the hill to the sprawling old house. White electric candles shone from the windows, and brown-bag luminaries lined the circular drive.

Uncle Ed supervised the brown-bag operation. He directed big and little hands in filling the paper bags half full of sand and in carefully anchoring the candles.

At twilight we all gathered at the top of the driveway and held our breath as Grandpa created magic by going from bag to bag lighting the candles.

No one said a word. We cherished the moment.

"Sons [and daughters] are a heritage from the LORD, children a reward from him. Like arrows in the hands of a warrior are sons born in one's youth. Blessed is the man whose quiver is full of them" (Psalm 127:3–5).

That was Grandpa's favorite verse. He quoted it Christmas Eve as we all gathered around Grandma's ninety-five-year-old table that had belonged to her grandmother.

It took all six table leaves, two of the longest tablecloths Grandma could buy, and every chair in the house, but we all fit—all sixteen of us.

From Alabama, Illinois, New York, and just the other side of the hill—we all came to be together, to hear our father read, and to watch our mother light the candles in the center of our Christmas Eve communion table.

From his well-worn Bible, Dad would read: "This do in remembrance of me . . ."

"Because God loves you and I love you, I give you this bread, this drink." Dad said it to the person on his left, and the message continued around the table.

Five or sixty-five—age didn't matter at this setting. We were drawn together by the common blood running through our veins and by that which ran from the cross.

Grandpa prayed. Some of us wiped away tears. Others held hands under the table. The men cleared their throats.

As we ate our traditional cream of potato soup, homemade rye bread, and Grandma's special Christmas salad that looked like a glowing candle, we knew we had experienced true kinship.

But most of all, we celebrated—as the men and boys fixed Christmas breakfast, as Uncle Daryl played Bach and Beethoven on the old player piano, as Denny read excerpts from his seminary dissertation.

The afternoon of Christmas day ushered in amateur hour. Nine-year-old Jori, adorned in a long dress and a shawl from Grandma's attic, made her organ debut with "Jingle Bells" and "Deck the Halls."

Three-year-old Jonathan introduced his new Ernie and

Bert puppets, one on each hand, and gave us his rendition of "Sesame Street." Uncle Mark set up the projector and transported us to old grist mills and clear mountain streams.

Uncle Ed played folk tunes on the mountain dulcimer he had made, and Grandpa read from his ageless book of verse and poetry. He remembered my favorites, the ones I begged him to read when I was only six and still sitting on his lap. Grandma donned an old-fashioned pilgrim's dress. Holding the children spellbound with her gentle voice, she read "The Courtship of Miles Standish."

I read my most recent story, one about visiting a crippled children's hospital, and Aunt Mary Ann served us her Flan Küchen, a fruit pastry she'd learned to make during her student year in Germany. Then we all leaned back and breathed deeply.

In the quietness, we could count the ticks on the mantel clock. Suddenly we were all children again. One by one, we had offered our gifts to each other. They were not wrapped in silver paper and red bows, but in the diverse talents and personalities that combine to make our family a reservoir of entertainment and fascination.

Another Christmas celebration had come and gone. From it we had drawn a storehouse of memories that would carry us until next year.

We found security in knowing that next year the old white house on the hill with its red sign on the door would welcome us, that the mantel clock would still be ticking, that Grandpa would light the luminaries, serve communion, and secretly tuck goodies into children's stockings.

Another oak log crumbles through the fireplace grate as our fire burns low.

I stand and shake myself from my reveries. Then I

glance at the children, wrapped in their sleeping bags, sound asleep, and Mark, dozing on the couch.

No. We can't live in the past. Things change. Children grow up. New family units emerge. Time for new traditions.

But what about the traditions that still live? Why bury them before they're dead?

I hear Grandma's old mantel clock. I smell her bread and taste her thick, savory cream of potato soup.

But that was then. This is now. What about my home, my family, our traditions?

I move listlessly through the last moments of the evening. I fill the stockings with miniature treasures, check the turkey, put another log on the fire, and join my sleeping family.

Families were meant to be together, I think as I wait for sleep. Suddenly I understand my Christmas Eve feelings of loss.

Even more important than memories of brown-bag luminaries, caroling, snowball fights, and the Hollinger amateur hour are the people of those memories. Our people. Our family extended.

I close my eyes and see their faces. Little do I know that next Christmas one face will be missing—that we will live with only memories of when we were a family of sixteen.

In years to come, it will always be our people— Grandma, Grandpa, aunts, uncles, cousins—that will call us home again.

Next year, next year for sure, we'll go home for Christmas.

CHAPTER SIX

The Mystery
of Friends

The Alabama Connection

We have little in common. My skin is white; theirs dark. I live in a white, five-room frame house down the blacktopped road. They live in a row of red-tile hovels, each with two rooms, a front and back door, cement floor, and a small fireplace for heating in winter. My house has indoor plumbing; their only source of water is the creek that runs past the far end of Mr. Huxley's turpentine still. I wear hand-smocked cotton frocks. They wear hand-me-downs made from flour sacks; size and shape don't matter. Sometimes Mr. Huxley brings yard goods from town and sells them at the commissary. Then mothers sew, and the clothes are passed through the community for generations to come. My daddy builds churches and preaches sermons. Their daddies work in the woods all day, tapping the pines for the resinous sap.

But here we are, a union of opposites, walking

together down the dusty Alabama truck trail that cuts through the middle of the turpentine still. We are partaking of place, their place, a school where they write on a long, wobbly table and sit for six hours on backless benches. They are proud to have a visitor sit with them on their benches. They don't mind that their school is also their church on Sunday or that the outside looks exactly like the red tile of their homes.

Later we push into the inner sanctum of their community, past the dense undergrowth that lines the creek. Here mothers wash clothes and children take Saturday afternoon baths. We hunt for tadpoles and carry them home in tin cans.

We stop by the commissary. Someone buys an Eskimo Pie, breaks it into fourths, and hands me the largest piece. Though I'm an outsider, I share with them the elements of life.

White folks didn't visit turpentine stills in those days. Black folks didn't take you in. But that day they did. They'd never seen me before; they knew only that my daddy had buried Aunt Kora's son. Aunt Kora was white, but she lived next door and bought her supplies at the commissary. Black and white folk alike all loved Aunt Kora.

Today, years later, the red-tile hovels still stand, but the people are gone. I drive by to see what the years have done, and I remember that "I was a stranger and [they] invited me in" (Matthew 25:35). What higher praise could be given any person, any community?

What Mr. Mansey Taught (Besides Biology)

Some things about high-school biology class I'd rather not remember. I have vague impressions of frogs and formaldehyde, platelets and amoebas, and other sights and smells I've tried to forget. But over the years since Bio 101, I've realized that I learned something I'm glad I didn't forget. It had nothing to do with science, though. It had to do with friendship.

Emily and I shared a lab table, but our friendship didn't begin with disected frogs and microscopes. I thought I knew her pretty well. She was a transparent kind of friend. I could tell, for example, how she and her mom were getting along by the way she answered the phone. And her driving style after school told me how her biology exam had gone eighth period.

Biology was Emily's barometer. A test score of 98 or above sent her soaring. Ninety-seven or below plunged her into despair. Emily never left any doubt about how she felt. I admired her for her honesty, so I put up with her mood swings.

My approach worked for a while. I'd either ignore Emily's lows or try to talk her into getting more sleep the next night. If I waited, her mood leveled out. Our friendship didn't require explanations or analysis. I left those kinds of exercises to the adult population. Friendship was for fun, not for psychoanalysis. I had never talked about my own feelings or been particularly concerned that others know what they were, so I didn't think it was important to explore someone else's.

Sometimes, however, I could not dismiss Emily's feelings so easily. One day I walked into the biology lab and found her sitting by the trash can vigorously ripping pages out of her blue biology notebook and, with equal vigor, depositing them in the large circular file beside the door. I knew those pages represented hours of careful, agonizing research for an assignment due in three weeks.

"This project is a total dud," Emily sputtered between the rips. "And to think I really believed I could be a biologist someday." She didn't bother to look at me when she said it.

It took a minute before it hit me that she was dumping half a quarter's worth of research. I tried a last-minute salvage job.

"Emily, listen to me, you've worked for weeks on that research. That's great stuff. I've read some of it. You are terrific in this class. If you had biology grades like mine you'd have reason for despair."

My words had little effect. The ripping continued. As

WHAT MR. MANSEY TAUGHT

I stood by helplessly and watched, Emily resolutely destroyed her biology project.

"Come on, Ruth. You know this is no good. Sloppy work. No conclusions. Even my experiment flopped. Some scientist."

By this time her behavior had started to irritate me. It made no sense. She knew she was good at biology. I knew she was good at biology. Everyone in the class knew she was good at biology. In fact, she was Mr. Mansey's only hope for the future from the entire sophomore class. She had come close to winning a science scholarship that usually went only to seniors. I took it as my moral obligation, in the name of friendship, to set her facts straight.

"Emily, you're at the top in biology. You know that. What's the deal? Mr. Mansey never said your project had to be perfect, though yours probably is. Here, let me help you get it out of the trash."

That was one step too far. "Just let me alone, Ruth!" She had never said that to me before. I was stunned. What should I do? Keep on coaxing her? Leave? Stand around and wait for her mood to shift? Step between her and the trash can and dig her report out as fast as she tossed it in?

As I stood there in indecision, Mr. Mansey returned from a faculty meeting. I saw him at the door and rushed over.

"Mr. Mansey. Emily just dumped her project," I blurted out like a three-year-old tattling on her friend. "She says it's not good enough. I think it's terrific."

I waited for Mr. Mansey to pick up my theme. Instead he pulled up a lab stool, sat down, and pushed his glasses up on his nose—the way he always did when deep in thought. For a long time he did not speak.

I felt a critical need for words right then, not silence.

Mr. Mansey apparently felt otherwise, but at last he cleared his throat.

"Emily, not getting that scholarship was a big disappointment to you, wasn't it? I guess I wasn't aware that it meant so much to you. You're feeling that the committee was unfair, aren't you?"

His words were magic. Emily spun around on her lab stool, laid her empty blue notebook on the table, lifted her head high, and looked straight into Mr. Mansey's face.

"Yes," she said spiritedly, "that committee was terribly unfair. They penalized me for being a sophomore."

I listened in amazement as Emily's pent-up hurt came pouring out, this time in words, not actions. I'd had no idea she felt so deeply about losing the scholarship. I only knew she had been sort of mopey the last day or two. I never thought to connect the two, even though she had told me all about the scholarship, her application, the committee interview, and finally about the rejection. I hadn't thought about what it would feel like to lose something you really had your heart set on.

Years have passed since sophomore biology, but I've thought frequently about Mr. Mansey. He may not have taught me much about biology, but he taught me a lesson about friendship I'll never forget. I learned that facts, no matter how true, are not always the best help for frustration, discouragement, or hurt feelings. Sometimes all people need is the assurance that we know and care about how they feel.

'Tis Better to Have Loved and Lost

Joan was all I ever wanted in a friend—fun, pretty, loving, fresh, creative, intelligent. We found each other in the crowded confusion of registration line on the first day of camp. Something about her made her stand out from the other 200 new faces around me—some mysterious chemistry between us made me feel as if she were a friend from long ago and we were just picking up where we had left off.

During the week an invisible magnet pulled Joan and me together. We went out of our way for each other. She dropped by my cabin on her way to the swimming pool, even though the pool was in the opposite direction. When I ended up at the back of the lunch line, she forfeited her up-front spot so she could stand and talk with me. I gave up horseback riding to go canoeing with her.

Whether sitting around a campfire, watching movies in the pavilion, or listening to a speaker in chapel, I always reserved the seat next to me for Joan. She produced a warm, secure, happy feeling in me. I felt safe with her. I could bring her into my room without having to clean up the mess. She didn't probe areas I was not yet willing to open for public inspection. I trusted her, even with my closed doors and closets.

Joan and I never had to work at conversation. We talked about the past and our dreams for the future. But we talked mostly about the present—boys and dates, which kind of pop we liked best and why, how stupid we thought the summer fashions were, whether dew rises or falls, where sand dollars come from, why paddling a canoe works better when you kneel. Sometimes we didn't even talk. Just being together was enough.

The last day of camp was like a funeral. I had known Joan for only seven days, yet we'd shared a lifetime. But now she was heading back to Florida, and I was going home to Alabama. I carried her suitcase to the bus, waved good-by, and watched the trail of dust disappear down the road. Joan and I never crossed paths again.

When the week ended, a puzzle that fit perfectly was torn apart. I had to pick up the pieces and start all over again. Walking the beach and watching the ocean, I felt the waves inside myself—restless, changing, tumbling all over each other. When I desperately wanted things to stay the same, the ebb and flow of change brought emptiness and the pain of separation.

I don't know why good friends and good times come and go; why God made tides that ebb and flow, waves that never crash in exactly the same spot, sand that shifts. I don't understand why seasons come and go; why lovely green trees shed their leaves to show ugly gray branches;

why the crimson red tulip has to die before it can bloom again; why the warm south winds swing around and blow cold air from the north.

What do I do with the season past? Discard it on a heap with all the other disposable, easy-come-easy-go commodities of our society and live as though life has no past or future? Should I never again venture into someone's life? I won't miss what I've never known. I'll never hurt if I never love.

Through the kaleidoscope of change I look for meaning and find that God has a purpose for every season of my life. And if God has a purpose, I am free to love even though camp ends in seven days; or graduation is only nine months away; or my neighbor may move in a year. I can reach out and embrace a new friendship without fear that it may soon end. Through it God wants me to learn, love, receive, give. I can let my roots sink deeply into the soil even though the deeper they go, the harder it will be to pull them up someday.

When things change and God turns over the well-worked soil of my experience, I know a new growing period is about to begin. That's how God works in his world, a world that never stays the same.

Martha's House

Martha's house is no longer warm. It used to be a haven for me. On cold winter days, her kitchen meant a cup of hot Swiss Mocha Coffee and a blueberry muffin fresh from the oven. We would sit by the window, sip our coffee, and watch yellow finches play tag in the fir tree.

Martha's house meant people. The gold embossed guest book, always open on the table at the top of the stairs, was filled with names and addresses of people from all over the world. When I pulled into her double driveway, someone almost always had arrived ahead of me.

Today I have the driveway to myself. I pull in beside a pile of discarded plywood, a rusted bucket, and half a garden hose. The kitchen window is covered by a piece of plywood, and the fir tree is a blackened stub.

I listen for the sounds of Martha's house—the mellow ticking of the grandfather's clock that marked the hours with a chime, the chug of the electric train that weaved through the basement and entertained my ten-year-old. Voices of celebration—an engagement dinner for her son. Voices of study—forty college students jammed into the living room for discipleship classes. Sounds of a patio picnic. Sounds of a missionary home from Spain. Happy sounds. Home sounds. I listen, but all I hear today is the 9:20 commuter as it pulls into the station three blocks away. Martha's house stands cold and silent, like a stone monument against the gray sky.

The fire did its work while everyone was away. All it left was the shell—a house without a home.

"Why Martha's house?" I shake my head in disbelief as I survey the scene. "Why? When her house belonged to everyone. Why? When she gave it so generously?" As I stand and grieve over a blackened building, ashes of happy memories, I remember the words of missionary Jim Elliott, who died on the beaches of Ecuador: "He is no fool who gives what he cannot keep to gain what he cannot lose." I know Martha has kept what she will never lose. Hospitality is not contained within four walls. The spirit of Martha's house will live on, even though the shell has been destroyed.

Sara

I could not help but notice the tall, gracious, grand-motherly type woman checking groceries. Usually I read magazine covers as I stand and wait my turn, but that day I watched Sara. She seemed to be genuinely enjoying the people she served, and everyone who left her counter was smiling. As I moved closer, I heard her Southern accent and was immediately taken in, my Southern roots stirred.

I read her name tag, then called her by name. She responded warmly and asked about my day. As the frozen orange juice and Raisin Bran moved down the conveyor belt, I learned that she was from South Carolina, that she attended the University of Georgia, and that she was leaving in two weeks to visit her daughter in New York.

The conversation ended too soon.

"Have a good day, Ruth," she said, pronouncing the

benediction on me as I stuffed the receipt into my purse and headed toward the door.

Apparently she read my name on my check. I was impressed that she bothered to notice.

After that day, I always looked for Sara when I was in that store. I waited for her line even if others were open. We talked about the Christmas crafts she was making, the spring flowers she was planting, or her vacation to South Carolina. Yet we still managed to get my groceries checked out and bagged without holding up the line.

One day, almost a year after we met, she told me that she and her husband attended our church and that she had known all along who I was.

Today I stare at the newspaper headlines in shock. The face of my friend Sara smiles at me from the upper right-hand corner of the page. The headline says: "Dead of gunshot wounds." I read the story four times, as though to convince myself, yet still I am not convinced. My friend Sara, murdered? My brain needs more time to absorb the reality.

I struggle with my hurt. Would I have been better off never to have learned her name or that she loved daffodils and crocheted snowflakes at Christmas? I would not be suffering as much today if she had remained "Check-out clerk. Aisle 4. Person unknown."

But in my grief for Sara I've come to understand anew that to care about people is a heavy cross to bear. It is the cross Christ chose, and for me, his follower, it is a cross that brings pain, yes, but also richness and reward. Today I have the memory of a beautiful woman who checked out groceries, enjoyed life, and loved the Lord genuinely.

To a Friend in Pain

Today you cannot pray for
Yourself.
So I will pray for you.
Your load is too great;
It suffocates your spirit
So that you have not
Even the breath to offer your
Burden to God.
So I will lift it up for you.

Today you cannot see God.
He's lost in the blackness,
Taken a midnight flight.
So I will come to you instead.
You cannot hear his voice,
But you can hear mine.
You cannot feel his touch,
But you can feel mine.
You have no hope;
Despair has conquered
For a while.
Your days stretch before you
Like the movement of a sad
Procession
On its way to an unknown grave.
You move without expectancy
On this silent march.
You see no end to the road.

No end.
No road.
No eyes to notice.
So I will notice for you.
I will see the signs of progress you
Cannot see,
Anticipate the sun
Before it comes up,
Praise tomorrow
Before I set my alarm tonight.
Because tomorrow you will need
Signs of progress,
Anticipation,
Praise.
Because tomorrow
You will feel
Signs of regression,
Fear,
Laments.
Let me be your song,
Your sunrise,
The blank check
For your depleted resources.
"Peace I leave you . . .
Not as the world giveth . . ."
I had neither the peace
Nor the power to find it.
"Here. Let Me help you.
I can do for you
What you cannot do for yourself."
So he sent rain to my dried-up
Reservoir,
Restored my soul
So that today
I can be strong for you.

Alien Turf

I know of a man who walked the city streets in a pair of ratty gym shoes and a soot-gray flannel shirt. His eyes were gray too—steel gray, like the massive iron girders that hold skyscrapers aloft and pin tenement buildings to the sky. Those steel eyes could make angry men back off and make lonely children feel welcome.

As the man walked the streets in his ratty gym shoes and gray flannel shirt, he watched and listened. He saw beyond the boarded-up windows of empty store fronts. He followed the noises up narrow stairs and into desolate rooms. There he found people. People angry over absentee landlords who sat in comfortable suburbs while rats chewed on tenants; people bitter about a system that handed out menial jobs, then took all the money they earned. People too tired to fight, too desperate to hope, too crushed to care.

As he walked among people of the cold and concrete, he found their escapes. He went with them into the places where tall glasses and pretty faces helped them forget—at least for a while. He knew how they felt when they stumbled into the emptiness of night. He was there in his ratty gym shoes and gray flannel shirt to steady them.

"You get too close and you'll get yourself killed," someone told him. He knew about their switchblades and Saturday night specials. He knew the hookers and pushers. But he invaded their turf anyway. He climbed over nine-foot fences to get to them. He ignored "Keep Out" signs.

His ratty gym shoes pounded the pavement with theirs as they maneuvered a basketball down back streets and alleys. He followed them to police stations, courts, and detention homes. "You give and they'll suck the blood right out of you," someone said. But he used his own money to pay their bail.

Others had come to the city before. They came in 280Z's, parked in the city parking garage, and caught the bus to the southside. They wore Adidas shoes and Christian Dior shirts. They brought new basketballs and hockey sticks donated by HUD or the YMCA. They came with handbook ideas on how to heal the insides of a city. When they'd made their visits, played their games, and distributed their literature, they brushed the city from their shoes and headed for the suburbs in their sports cars. And no one in the city had heard a word they said.

But when the man with the steel-gray eyes spoke, the people heard. When he knocked on doors, people let him in. And when someone ran a bullet through his head while he slept in his three-by-five tenement room, a rich suburban father grieved.

The people of the street asked, "If he had known we'd kill him, would he have come?" Some said yes. They'd heard him talk about another Man who had gone willingly to work among people he knew would kill him.

The Word became flesh and made his dwelling among us (John 1:14).

CHAPTER SEVEN

The Mystery
of Strangers

The Remarkable Mr. Per

Somewhere in Wisconsin lives a man named Mr. Per. The license plates on his Winnebago told us where he was from, and he told us a few other facts: he was married, he liked to fish, and he had a Persian cat named Puff. Everything else we learned about him we found out by watching.

We first spotted Mr. Per as we backed our van into campsite seven along the south shore of Bear Lake in northern Wisconsin. As we drove in, his red flannel shirt disappeared through the white birch and pine that separated our parking spot from his. "Somebody's raked our spot," Jori said, struggling with a tent pole. Sure enough, we spotted fresh rake marks in the dirt. Later we saw a rake leaning against the Winnebago.

When we returned from our after-dinner walk, we

found a pile of logs stacked neatly beside our fireplace and two coloring books with crayons on the picnic table.

"Somebody likes kids," Mr. Per said quietly the next morning when I mentioned the coloring books. I knew they were from him, but I didn't press for a confession.

The next night our lantern was lit when we made our way up the path from the lake. He had hung it in perfect position to light the rocky way we had to walk. A bouquet of wildflowers in a paper cup sat on our table. As we walked into camp, we heard Mr. Per whistling through the woods, heading toward his site.

"What a nice man," Nicky commented, burying his nose in the sweet smell of cornflower and goldenrod.

The next day, we saw Mr. Per pushing through the pines toward the park bathrooms, rubber gloves, bucket, mop, and ammonia bottle in hand.

Mr. Per's graciousness knew no end. Nine-year-olds can be a hazard in a fisherman's boat, but Mr. Per invited Nicky to go fishing with him anyway. I awoke to the sound of oars on water just outside the tent. I watched as old man and youth glided across the sheet of morning sun, then anchored in the middle of the motionless lake. Nothing stirred except my heart. Who was Mr. Per, I wondered. A banker? Lawyer? Garbage collector? College professor? Auto mechanic? I didn't know, but it didn't matter. I had never met anyone who said so much about himself in so few words.

Later, Mr. Per showed Nicky how to clean the trout and cook them in a pan over the fire. Nicky proudly served us fresh fish for dinner.

On Friday we waved good-by as Mr. Per and his wife left for their next campsite. State parks were a hobby with them. I wondered who their next neighbors would be.

We did not soon forget Mr. Per. For the next few days

his name came up often in conversations. By the shores of Bear Lake, our lives had been touched by a simple man who knew something profound about service. Mr. Per demonstrated for us what Jesus taught about the true spirit of giving: "But when you give . . . do not let your left hand know what your right hand is doing, so that your giving may be in secret. Then your Father, who sees what is done in secret, will reward you" (Matthew 6:3–4).

Mr. Per's kind of giving stood out to me because I live in a world of performances acted for an audience. It's easy for me to take on the same kind of role. Life too easily becomes a stage where I play out my deeds of mercy to receive personal rewards—approval, admiration, visibility. How often do I write articles, give speeches, perform the duties of parenthood, and then wonder if anyone notices how well I'm doing? Is it true mercy if I visit the grieving mother down the block and casually tell about it the next time I'm with a friend? If I take a potted plant to a woman trapped in her own apartment, afraid of the outside world, and then make her the subject of my next article, have I truly served at all, or has the result become more important than the service? Am I serving, not for what it does for the other person, but for what it does for me?

When Jesus defined giving, he singled out for criticism the religious types obsessed with public displays of service and showed them a higher standard. When he healed the deaf and dumb man, he commanded onlookers to keep quiet about what they'd seen. He often repeated the request as he moved across the countryside bringing health and wholeness. He, too, lived in a day of performers. The crowds wanted pageantry and kingdoms. He patiently reminded them that he had come for more than publicity and fanfare.

Vernon Walters, former ambassador to the United

Nations, once said, "There is no end to the amount of good that can be done when one is not concerned with who gets the credit."

Mr. Per gave, I believe, not for the satisfaction of being known, but for the satisfaction of giving. I wonder, would I be so quick to serve if no one ever knew? Would I rake a campsite, stack firewood, light a lantern—then go whistling through the dark before anyone ever had a chance to say "Thanks, we knew all along it was you."

The Food Pantry
That Talked

I stand in the checkout line
at the grocery store. Bored,
as usual. I rearrange the items, making sure that the bread
is on top of the orange juice and that all the cans have the
labels right side up. Then I flip through a *Country Living*
magazine.

A screeching noise ahead of me ends my boredom. Up
and down the checkout lines, heads turn. Apparently the
woman at the head of the line is unaware that her voice
carries across several checkout counters.

I spot the targets of her hostility—two young teenage
girls, apparently her daughters, with ghetto blasters held
up to their ears. They stare blankly, straight ahead,
transported by their music to some other place.

"Put those horrible things down so I can talk to you,"

the woman orders. The ghetto blasters do not move, but the mother continues her monologue.

"I tell you, this is the last time you ever come to the store with me. Put those things down." The radios move slightly. "You two are never satisfied, always wanting more. I'm sick and tired of your selfish attitude. Sick and tired of you. Do you hear?"

One daughter, with stooped shoulders, straight hair, and acne, nods slightly. The other glares at her mother, then looks around to see if anyone is watching. Her face flushes beet red when she realizes we are. She turns her back to her mother and faces the candy rack.

The radios go back up to their ears, but the mother continues as she unloads the cans from her cart.

"You girls need to go live in Bangladesh. Then you'd learn to appreciate what I do for you. Patty, turn that radio down and don't tell me to shush."

I want to take the girls and hide them under my coat where bitter words cannot wound. I want to tell them they're okay. The one with acne looks ready to crawl under the counter. The other still has her back toward her mother.

The woman lines her cans, exactly a dozen of each item, neatly on the conveyor belt. I wish she took such care with her daughters. Tomatoes, green beans, sweet potatoes, corn, peas, peaches, pears, spaghetti, beef stew. All arranged according to label.

She turns to the clerk, and her voice turns low and sweet. "All this food is for our missionaries. I'm in charge of the food pantry at our church. Our people give so generously. We have a real ministry."

Emotion tightens my throat. Is it anger? Pity? Righteous indignation? Embarrassment for missionary pantries around the world?

As I watch her go out the door with her precious cargo, two pained teenagers in tow, I remember God's sentiments as he pronounced judgment on a hypocritical Israel. "For I desire mercy, not sacrifice, and acknowledgment of God rather than burnt offerings" (Hosea 6:6).

I line up my groceries on the black conveyor belt and silently pray that causes will never become more important to me than people—especially the people I love most.

Garage Attendants Don't Come Up Here

The sixth level of the O'Hare International Airport parking garage feels more like the Sahara desert today. The sun presses down on me as I push my luggage cart rapidly along, eager for the relief of my Datsun's air conditioning. After a long day, home is uppermost in my mind. I finally reach the car, deposit my luggage in the back, and buckle myself into the driver's seat for the trip home. I turn the key, expecting a stream of cool air to relieve me within minutes from these oven-like conditions. But nothing happens. I turn the key again. Still no response. No matter how I turn the key, pump the clutch, or shift the gears, the car remains still. My Datsun has died.

Not only does it feel like the Sahara, it might as well be the Sahara. I look around for signs of life, but the only things moving are jets that streak toward the sun every sixty seconds or so. Few people park on the outer aisles of level six in the middle of the week. I look around for a button to push to summon help, but all I see are solid concrete pillars. I don't know where else to search for help.

Just then I spot a man walking the outer aisle, looking as though he has nowhere in particular to go. I wonder why he's roaming a 90-degree cement desert at mid-afternoon. He comes toward me, and I notice his red and white airport security badge. Ten years of parking in this garage and I've never seen an airport security guard.

"I don't know this territory," he says when I ask him where I might find a mechanic. "I never come up here."

I begin to feel the drama unfolding. *If you never come up here, why are you here?* I wonder, but I don't ask because I think I know the answer.

Though young, he seems to know cars. He goes deliberately to the life centers under the hood. Battery. Cables. Fluid. Belts. Plugs. "In this car the ignition is underneath," he says as he slides under the car, white shirt and all. "I believe it's your battery." His diagnosis is complete, but the only movement is still in the skies. Sweat drips from us both. "I have no idea where you'll find cables." He slams the hood in a kind of benediction. He's done all he can do. He will go on collecting luggage carts, and I will be left alone in my cement desert.

We stand for a moment in silent contemplation. Out of the corner of my eye I see a yellow flash moving slowly toward the outer aisle. Ten years of parking in this garage and I've never once seen flashing yellow. "Perfect timing," says the youth with the red badge. He waves to the brown truck with the flashing yellow light. I read "Free battery charging" on the tailgate as the vehicle of mercy pulls to a stop.

"Yes. Perfect timing," I say to him. To myself I say, *I am loved.*

"What are you doing up here?" the man behind the wheel asks the security guard.

"I don't know. Just happened to be up here collecting carts. I am a bit far from my station. Guess I needed some sun."

I know what you're doing up here, I say to myself as my engine comes to life and I wave my thanks.

Today I feel God's love. Tomorrow's dilemmas may not be so easily solved. There may be no security guard to come to my rescue. On days I do not feel God's presence, I will remember today. And if tomorrow I cannot thank God for the present, I will look back to a 90-degree day in an airport garage and thank him for the past.

The Wanderer

He wanders up and down the narrow road,
Walking the shoulder,
Always hugging the shoulder,
His long, black hair trailing in the
Wind.
Cars whiz by; we wonder,
Whose son?
Where's he going?
Where's he been?
Maybe
He doesn't even know
For sure.
But he does.
He walks in the dust
With determined step,
Swinging his arms as he goes,
In tune with something
Or someone,
Pausing here and there
To talk to the clouds,

To swing on the goalposts
That mark the end of the field,
To pick a branch from a scrubby
Roadside shrub.
Twice he crosses the same
Parking lot
To cool himself at the
Tastee-Freeze.
Surrounded by ice-cream floats
And frosty root beers,
He only breathes the air

And goes out the door again,
His mission unknown
Except to him.
But I try to guess.
Brilliant scientist
Whose mind overdosed on facts?
A mother's son
Who didn't quite fit?
Society's reject
Tossed aside to his own illusions?
He looks both ways,
Wipes the sweat from his brow
With a big, red handkerchief,
Ties it around his wrist,
And takes to the road again.
I watch his solitary stride,
Facing the traffic head on.
He disappears from sight,
But folks say he will come again.
And I wonder
Who he is.
If he knocks on the door of an inn,
Would anyone let him in?
Did anyone let Him in?
Did anyone understand who He
Was?
Or did they wonder too?

The Lily and the Dark

 I manage to read the apartment numbers even though the hall is dark. The door I am looking for is 307. I take a deep breath, shift the Easter lily to my left hand, and knock. I don't know what to expect on the other side, and I'm not sure I'm prepared for whatever it is. A request in the mail has brought me here on this day before Easter. A new Christian who lives far away is concerned for her aunt who fears the outside world. She has not left her apartment alone for five years.

The door opens, allowing a sliver of light to come through. Above the chain lock I see a face. I feel I am looking into a cage. I speak her name softly, then her niece's name and my own, reminding her that I called the previous night to say I would be coming. She shows no sign of remembering, but when I repeat her name she reaches up and unbolts the door.

I walk into a tomb, of sorts. A cold room full of shadows. She doesn't turn on a lamp. I can make out a crucifix hanging between two baskets of plastic flowers on the opposite wall. The TV gives off light but no sound. I put the Easter lily on the coffee table next to a framed picture of Christ on the cross. Rosary beads drape the frame. My lily looks out of place, but I don't know where else to set it.

We skip the polite formalities. She suspects I am here for a reason. "I don't have nothing to do with religion. It made me sick. Every time I prayed, I cried; I felt so guilty. Ended up in a psych hospital. Doctors told me not to pray anymore." She seems to fade into the dusk and then suddenly reappear.

"You're not one of those born-again ones, are you? I have no time for them. My sister stole my husband. Now she comes wanting to talk to me about being born again. No sir. You can keep that born-again stuff."

She doesn't wait for a response. While she talks I sit silently in a green overstuffed chair thinking I might as well *be* the chair. Every now and then I speak, but she makes it clear that she wants to do the talking.

"It's been eight years since I've seen two of my children. One comes every month, brings my groceries, sets them on the table, then leaves." I notice a shelf of pictures in gold frames—apparently the closest she comes to having relationships.

After listening for an hour and a half, I feel as if I have walked through a Greek tragedy. The dark is settling in, but we are still without a light in the room. In the dusk I see the lily. It still looks out of place.

When I rise to go I ask if I might pray. She doesn't object but starts to cry in the middle of my prayer.

"Please come back. Please be my friend." She holds

tightly to my hand. I promise to come again. On the way to the door I pass the crucifix. The thought occurs to me that Easter has not yet come to this place. Christ is still on the cross. She lives without hope.

The door closes behind me. She returns to the prison of her mind, and I walk out into the soft April evening. The sky is spread with stars. I think of the one who came to "set the captives free."

No, the lily is not out of place in apartment 307. It's exactly where it belongs. Oh that I might walk more often among the captives. For in so doing, we both learn about freedom.

Garfield

I could tell he was nervous when he entered the plane. A purple half-shirt covered part of his body, long blond hair screened most of his face, and sunglasses covered his eyes. They hid his identity, but not his anxiety.

"I'm on my way to the Garfield School in Denver," he announced loudly to the flight attendant as he entered the aircraft just ahead of me.

"You ever heard of the Garfield School?" the bemused stewardess asked me.

"Can't say that I have. The only Garfield I know is a cat." We both laughed.

Those of us who wore navy suits and carried burgundy briefcases shared a certain camaraderie. We had little in common with anyone who wore purple half-shirts and a single black leather glove with the fingertips cut off.

While the rest of the passengers settled in, Garfield walked the aisles.

"Could you find a window seat for me?" he asked the flight attendant. "I think I might get sick if I can't see out."

By now, Garfield had captured the full attention of the passengers. We looked on, amused.

"Garfield wants to know where the smoking section is." A second flight attendant entered the drama. Apparently word had spread about Garfield.

His next trip up the aisle was to ask for help with his straw bag, which was too big to fit under the seat. He had planned on holding it, he said. Couldn't understand how holding it would hurt anyone. The straw bag ended up under the seat.

The flight attendant wiped her forehead as she returned to the bulkhead.

"The guy's never flown," she chuckled to those of us within earshot. "This could be interesting."

For me, the drama with Garfield started inside the terminal. The woman standing beside him looked old—much older than I guessed her age to be—and her gray hair poked out in all directions. During most of the thirty-minute wait she stood and stared at the DC-10 parked at the gate.

"What a bird," she muttered, as much to herself as to anyone. The purple shirt beside her never replied. Neither mother nor son seemed to notice anything but the plane. They spoke no other words to each other. When it came time to board, Garfield was one of the first in line.

The woman moved with him to the door. While some of us hugged and whispered tender good-bys to loved ones, Garfield's mother raised her hand to her son's shoulder.

Then, with more of a push than a hug, she pronounced her parental benediction. "Kid, you're on your own now."

She turned toward us.

"Finally, he's gone!" Her words came out in a long relieved sigh, as if it had been stored inside her for her son's lifetime. Garfield never looked back. He marched forward toward the big bird and Denver. He never even said good-by.

Hours later, as my children wrap their arms of "welcome home" around me, I remember Garfield. When did the mother-son silence start, I wonder. Long before the airport scene, no doubt. Probably over something inconsequential, like dust under his bed or purple half-shirts. Parent-child blowouts don't usually start with a loud bang. They begin as a small leak in communication.

"I'm so glad to be your mom," I say to the children as I tuck them into bed.

Someday I'll tell them the story of Garfield. But tonight we talk about the "king and queen" rock formations that I saw while flying over Monument Valley, about the goal Nicky scored in soccer, and about the B Jori got on her English test.

As I turn out their lights I think about a purple half-shirt, a black leather glove with fingers sticking out, and a mom who said, "Finally, he's gone." No wonder they had nothing more to say to each other.

Lessons From a Coffee Counter

Union Station looks as if it has never slept. The California Zephyr from San Francisco backs onto track 1, and the Burlington Commuter Line empties work-bound passengers on platform 7. The passageways are jammed. We arrive at the gates just in time to hear the announcement that the Broadway Limited from New York is an hour late. The kids head for the video arcade, quarters jingling in their pockets, and Mark and I grab the next two available stools at the coffee counter. All of Union Station, it seems, flows through this point. It's a people watcher's paradise.

I order my coffee black and my doughnut without sugar. The waitress sets my coffee in front of me and reaches under the counter for a spoon. "Thank you,

Thelma," I say as she heads the other way. At the sound of her name she spins around and looks me in the eye for the first time. "Not many people bother to read my nametag," she says. Her black face breaks into a broad grin as she goes to her next customer. In no time she is back, propping her elbows on the counter's edge as though she intends to stay.

"So you're a Bear's fan," Mark says, nodding at her navy stocking cap that proclaims, in bright orange, "This is Chicago Bear Country." She talks about her ten-year-old grandson who lives with her and watches every game. "I can't help but be a fan," she adds. "We watch together. Poor child has no one else."

Thelma refills our cups even though mine is still three-quarters full. She glances down the counter. "Yes, ma'am, I've been coming to this here corner for fifteen years now, every morning of the year at 5:30. Very few people like to talk. They too busy. But I could write a book about 'em. Maybe I will someday. Sure would be better than pouring coffee."

She shuffles down the row to collect her tips and wipe the counter. When she returns she tells us about her customer who pours jelly beans on his buttermilk pancakes every morning. And about the fur-wrapped woman who sat down one morning, looked at the menu, then asked, "Isn't this the Mademoiselle Dress Shop?" Thelma slaps the counter and laughs when she tells it. I notice a front tooth is missing.

The hour goes quickly. The children have returned, their quarters depleted. Thelma has talked and refilled our cups the entire time. We stand to leave when we hear the Broadway Limited announced on track 2. "You come back now," she says as she picks up Mark's generous tip. "And have a safe trip." I don't bother to tell her we aren't going anywhere.

As we look through the crowd for Grandma and Grandpa I think of all the Thelmas in the world. Each with stories to tell if only someone would ask. I think too of the man who sat one day near a well, the local watering hole, and took time to show an interest in the woman he met there (see John 4). I determine I will ask people questions more often.

Epilogue

I watch for you among the hurried travelers
Who push their luggage carts down F concourse
Toward the baggage claim.
You are here,
Among the crowd,
Perhaps standing by a coffee counter
Drinking hot tea with just a bit of cream.
Or stopping to buy stamps
To send messages to the ones you love.
This is your airport.
You travel it often.
You are here among us.
But you are not one of us.

I look for you among the clouds
That form just outside the window of the DC-10,
So close I think I can scoop them up
And take them home for our nature collection.
You have ridden these clouds
Circuited these winds
Scouted this vast expanse on which we hang.

This is your route.
You travel these airways.
You hide yourself among the clouds.
But you are higher than the clouds.

I look for you among the hills
Covered by Douglas fir
And redwood pine.
You have picked this rhododendron bloom
Traced this beetle in the sand
Felt this wind blow in your face.

This is your creation.
You walk these paths.
Yet, really, you walked only one path—
To a cross.

Lord,
The greatest paradox of all,
You are God
With us
But above us.
In us
But not of us.
A God I know
Yet above all knowing
Wrapped in mystery.
Worthy of praise.